W9-AAC-244

essential

FISHING

essential

FISHING

Everything You Need to
Catch the Big One

Ronnie Garrison

Adams Media
Avon, Massachusetts

To the memory of my mother, Vera Dunaway Garrison,
and her brothers Mayhu, Adron, J. D., and Roger
who all inspired my love of fishing

Published by Adams Media, an F+W Publications Company
57 Littlefield Street, Avon, MA 02322 U.S.A.
www.adamsmedia.com

ISBN: 1-59869-128-7

Printed by KHL Printing Co Pte Ltd, in Singapore.

J   I   H   G   F   E   D   C   B   A

Previously published as The Everything® Fishing Book
Copyright ©2003, F+W Publications, Inc.

Contents

Acknowledgments

Thanks to Jim Berry and his staff at Berry's Sporting Goods in Griffin Georgia, and Fritz Nordengren (✑ learning2fish@41) in my chat room and at New Media for Non Profits (✑ www.nmnp.org).

Top Ten Reasons
Why You'd Rather Be Fishing

1. Your job ties you up inside a stuffy office all day and you're feeling a desperate need to get back in touch with nature.

2. You are extremely fussy about eating only the freshest fish possible.

3. You want something to do with your kids that does not involve a television.

4. You've run out of fish stories and need some more!

5. You are sick of your spouse running off on fishing trips without you, leaving you home alone.

6. You think those hip waders look really spiffy.

7. You want more excuses to get on a boat.

8. The movie *Jaws* scared the heck out of you when you were ten, and now it's time for payback.

9. You've always wanted to know the difference between a crappie and a crappy fish.

10. You don't want to end up being like one of those stamp collectors!

Introduction

▶MILLIONS OF PEOPLE GO FISHING EVERY YEAR. They enjoy everything from a quiet afternoon sitting by a pond catching four-ounce bream to trolling miles offshore and battling 400-pound marlin. Some like the relaxing, contemplative aspects of fishing while others want the thrill of competitive fishing.

Fishing is not always about catching fish. Many fishing trips are considered a complete success because of time spent with family, the enjoyment of nature, or the relaxation of escaping from work. Catching fish certainly adds something more than good eating to a fishing trip, but you should never let your enjoyment of fishing depend on it.

There's something for everyone in the sport of fishing. You can start fishing with a minimal investment and start catching fish immediately, or you can go all out and buy fancy equipment and try for fish that require learning skills to get them to bite. No matter what your age, physical health, or income level, there is fishing that you can enjoy.

Join with friends and family members or fish all alone: the fish don't care, and you can do exactly what you want to do. There are benefits of fishing with others but solitude can be an important part of fishing as well. Take kids fishing with you on some trips and give them memories that they will always value. Go with a group of friends for some bonding time. Or solve all the problems of the world as you fish alone with no one to disturb your thoughts.

Although you don't have to catch fish, there's something special about the pull of a fighting fish on the end of your line. Most fishermen derive satisfaction in knowing they have solved the puzzle of what the fish want to bite and how to catch them. Even though people are a lot smarter than fish, you still have to learn their habits and figure out their reactions to catch them successfully. Solving this puzzle is a good feeling for many.

There are fishing opportunities all over the world. If you travel, you'll see people fishing everywhere you go if there's water. Joining them will give you an experience of their world and help you understand them. And if you want to get to know a stranger, go fishing with that person. You'll probably become friends.

This book gives you information you need to start fishing, from choosing equipment and finding a place to joining a group. If you're just starting out, the basics of fishing can be found here. If you've been fishing for many years there are tips and information here that should help you, too. Saltwater and freshwater information is included in every chapter.

In this hectic modern world, too many people don't take time to think about what they're doing. Fishing gives you a chance to slow down and consider things. One of the things you must consider is other fishermen, and some suggestions on being a good neighbor while fishing is included here. Think about other fishermen when you're making decisions on what to do on the water.

Welcome to the world of fishing. It's a sport that everyone can enjoy for a lifetime. Take some time to learn the basics and you'll be set to explore the more intricate fishing opportunities. You'll be able to find a type fishing that will suit you.

Chapter 1

The World of Fishing

Fishing has always been one of mankind's favorite pastimes. It can be as relaxing as a snooze in the shade or as thrilling as an explosion of water as a 1,000-pound marlin jumps at the end of your line. From contemplating a cork to casting for cash, there's some kind of fishing for everyone. And there's no better time to get started than right now.

The History of Fishing

Cavemen fished to get food to survive. Isaac Walton fished to contemplate the mysteries of life. Denny Brauer fished to win more than $1,000,000 on the bass tournament trail. Throughout history people have fished for many reasons, and some of those reasons are just as valid today as they ever were.

Prehistoric Fishing

Primitive civilizations fished for something to eat, not for the sport of it. They used whatever methods worked, from clubs and spears to crude traps. Their goal was to stay alive, so they didn't want the fish to fight; they just wanted to catch it.

American Indians fished for food and also used a variety of methods to get them. Although they also used weirs (a type of fishing trap), spears, and other methods to catch them, they also caught fish on hook and line. Crude J-shaped objects made from bone and flint have been found in drainage pits near Indian mounds. These objects seem to be early fish hooks, indicating these people may have actually been able to feel the fight of a fish on the end of a line. You can imagine an Indian sitting on the bank of a stream and smiling as a trout fought at the end of his sinew line and flint hook tied to a sapling pole. That may have been the beginning of sport fishing in the Americas.

At some point people started fishing for the enjoyment of catching fish, although their catch was still used as an important food source. But there are more efficient ways to catch fish than using a hook and line. There was something more to it than just gathering food.

From Food to Fun

It's easy to imagine that people found out they enjoyed fishing a lot more than gathering other kinds of food. As humankind became more efficient in gathering enough food to survive, more time was available to spend enjoying what they were doing.

The use of boats increased the range of fishermen and also gave them a way to get to inaccessible places in rivers, lakes, and coastal waters. Boats increased the efficiency of fishermen, allowing them to set nets and drive fish to weirs in deeper water. But they also gave early fishermen a way to get away from the bank to fish with hook and line.

Over many years equipment gradually changed to reflect the fact that fishermen wanted to have fun as well as catch dinner. Hooks made of iron were better than flint hooks and lines developed, from horsehair to woven flax fibers to catgut. The first lines were thrown by hand and probably wrapped around a stick. Reels to hold the line were developed and then were attached to poles. A slow, gradual improvement was made but fishing equipment really didn't change much for hundreds of years.

FACT

The first book about fishing written in English was the *Treatise of Fysshynge with an Angle* by Dame Juliana Berners. Written in 1496, it discusses angling, which is fishing with pole and line. It shows that by that time some people were fishing for sport and not just for sustenance.

Poles have been in use for a very long time but weren't common in Europe until the middle of the thirteenth century. Some drawings indicate reels may have been used as early as 3000 B.C. in China, long before being used anywhere else. By the beginning of the fourteenth century they were in use in Europe and made their way to North America soon after settlement began.

Beginning of Modern Fishing

From the early fourteenth century to the end of the nineteenth century there was a gradual improvement in fishing equipment. Most fishing was still for food but the upper class perfected fly-fishing and it became almost an art form. Rods made from bamboo and quality hand-made fly reels were the top-of-the-line in equipment.

The industrial age brought changes to fishing with better equipment, the advent of bait-casting reels and rods with guides for them, and better line. But the real changes started about the time of World War II with mass-produced rods and reels and a demand for them. New types of reels were also developed with spin-casting and spinning reels becoming popular. And new synthetic lines were first introduced, making fishing easier and more productive.

QUESTION?

When were reels first used for casting?
The first reels were used for holding line only, and the line was cast from the rod, as modern fly equipment. Not until the 1830s were reels capable of being used to cast a lure from the reel itself.

From the end of World War II until the late 1960s, rods, reels, and types of line improved faster than ever before in history. Prices got low enough that kids could buy decent equipment from their allowances. The numbers of people fishing increased as they had more leisure time. Fishing was considered a leisure activity and the fish brought home to eat were an added bonus.

Advent of Tournaments

In the late 1960s the first bass tournaments were held. These tournaments changed fishing in many ways, turning it from a relaxing, contemplative pastime into a fast-paced, competitive sport. As more and more fishermen demanded better equipment, changes started taking place rapidly.

During the next thirty years electronics were developed to allow fishermen to see what's underwater. Electric motors were improved and gas motors for boats became huge, high-powered engines that made newly designed boats fly on the water. Lures and plastic worms went through a tremendous change and became so popular most big discount stores dedicated more than one aisle to displaying them.

One of the biggest changes brought about by tournaments was making catch-and-release fishing popular. Although trout fishermen had long released fish they caught, the general public considered all caught fish as food. But tournament fishermen brought in large numbers of bass and they were not able to clean them all, so they were given away or wasted.

To combat the poor image of bass tournament fishermen wasting fish, catch and release became the way to go. Tournaments were set up to keep fish alive and put them back after weighing them. There are penalties for bringing in a dead fish. Today catch and release is almost a religion with some fishermen. They would never keep any fish to eat.

Game and Fish Departments of states and counties establish limits and regulations to control the numbers of fish taken. In many waters size limits are set to encourage fishermen to keep fish of certain sizes. Fisheries biologists say not only is it okay to keep fish to eat, sometimes it helps the fishing.

Why Fish

There are as many reasons to fish as there are fishermen. For some it's relaxing and a good way to sooth frayed nerves. For others it's an exciting, competitive sport that gets the adrenalin flowing. Some still fish for the food it puts on the table since fresh fish are by far the best. Parents taking kids fishing is a great way to develop a good relationship with them and keep kids out of trouble. You may fish for these reasons and may have other reasons of your own.

According to The American Sport Fishing Association:

- There are an estimated fifty million recreational anglers in the United States.
- Fishermen outnumber people who play tennis and golf combined.
- California, Florida, and Texas are the states with the highest numbers of fishermen.
- The economic impact of fish in the United States is over $100 billion.

Fishing is a very popular sport worldwide. Anyone can fish at any age, a factor that makes it a great pastime for anyone. Since so many people choose to fish there must be something to it. Maybe it is a sport for you to pursue.

Fishing for Food

Anyone who has eaten a shore lunch of fish caught, cleaned, and cooked all within the span of a few minutes raves about how great the fish taste. No store-bought fish can come close to being as good as ones so fresh. And you know where the fish came from and how they were handled.

ALERT!

Chemicals and other pollutants have contaminated fish from some waters. Check fishing regulations for warnings and advisories on eating fish from your area. You're often told not to eat fish from certain waters more than a set number of times per week or month. These limits are extremely conservative so you should be safe following them.

Fish you catch yourself can also be much cheaper than what you buy. There are methods of catching fish that don't require much money and produce a lot of good-tasting fish. Watch your spending on equipment and bait and you can be cost effective. Even better, consider the cost as part of your recreation budget and the fish as a free bonus.

Fishing for Sport

There's something magical about the pull of a fish at the end of your line. It's almost addictive, and once you feel it you want to experience it again and again. That's why people like to catch bigger and bigger fish—they fight harder than the smaller ones. The fight of the fish is also why sport fishermen tend to use the lightest equipment possible to accentuate the fight.

All fish can give you a good fight, from a little yellow perch on ultralight tackle to a big-game saltwater fish like marlin on the heaviest tackle around. Fish are available to almost everyone, so fishing is a sport most people can enjoy. For the young it's an almost instinctive urge to fish and enjoy the sport even at a very early age.

Many people are competitive and fishing can feed that spirit, too. Most folks like to fish with others and try to catch the most or the biggest fish. This is what led to tournament fishing with big money prizes. It's a challenge to try to outdo other fishermen near you. You get the same feeling as you do when the team you're on wins in any other sport.

Fishing for Relaxation

Watching a cork floating on the water, waiting for it to tremble and then disappear can be an exciting part of fishing, but nothing is more relaxing. When you're concentrating on that cork, watching it with eager anticipation, the worries of the world seem to go away. You're focused on one thing and nothing else will bother you during that time.

Build a fire, have a cooler of your favorite beverage and good snacks handy, and you can forget about the cares of the world. From sitting in the shade or basking in the sun to lying back under the stars, fishing is as peaceful as you want it to be.

If you have access to a boat you can sit or lie in it with some poles out and be gently rocked to sleep. And if someone accuses you of wasting time, just tell that person you're fishing. It's always a great excuse for doing nothing but enjoying life. You can do absolutely nothing and get away with it.

Teaching Children

There's an old saying "Give a man a fish, feed him for a day; teach a man to fish, feed him for a lifetime." This is true when taken literally but even more true when applied in a broader sense to children. Children who enjoy fishing are too busy to get into as much trouble as other kids. And they're learning a pastime that will last them a lifetime.

Fishing teaches young people patience, how to pay attention, and the rewards of doing something correctly. Kids take to fishing naturally, and kids and adults fishing together helps eliminate any generation gap. It can also help teach kids to save their money for a desired item like a new reel. Parents fishing with their children will be closer to them than those who don't take their children fishing.

Don't try to teach kids to be patient too fast. When you take kids fishing, especially young children, let them play. Don't get too serious. When they tire of fishing let them throw rocks, look for bugs, dig in the dirt, or anything else that will be fun for them.

Although some kids may get into trouble slipping into places to fish that are off limits to them, they're less likely to get into other kinds of trouble. Kids who fish seem to be less likely to experiment with drugs, join gangs, or commit crimes. Fishing just seems to help kids grow up right.

The Rewards of Fishing

The rewards of fishing include catching good food, enjoying peace of mind, and acquiring a pastime that will last you the rest of your life. The relationships you develop with fellow fishermen and children can be invaluable to you in the present and the future. And you'll never get bored or wonder what you can do with your spare time if you get involved in fishing.

You can get your whole family involved in fishing. Anyone can fish and it requires no special physical stamina or abilities that can't be learned. From toddlers to grandparents, people find that a fishing outing is a great way to get to know each other better. And spending time with your family is a great reward in itself.

There's a bumper sticker that says "Time spent fishing is not counted against you." Although meant to be humorous, it has a lot of truth in it. Fishing is so relaxing and such a good stress reliever that it can help your health. You often hear about old fishermen, and fishing helps them get that way. It's no coincidence that fishing is a major pastime of the characters in the movie *Grumpy Old Men*.

Fishing Has Negatives, Too

There are some drawbacks to fishing if you let them become a problem.

Any hobby or pastime can become a problem if you become fanatical about it, and fishing is no exception. Take fishing for what it is and don't try to make it substitute for things that might be missing in your life.

Fishing Can Be Time Consuming

Even if fishing doesn't obsess you, it can take a lot of time. Unless you're one of the lucky ones with a pond or stream in your backyard, you'll have to get your fishing gear together and go to the fishing spot. This can mean anything from a short walk to a very long drive. If you fish from a boat you'll have to keep it working right. And fishing gear always needs cleaning and repair.

It's very easy to lose track of time while fishing, too. A short trip can quickly develop into an all-day or all-night affair whether the fish are biting or not. If they're hitting good you won't want to leave, and if they are not biting you'll want to stay until they start.

The High Cost of Fishing

You can easily spend a tremendous amount on fishing. Many fishermen leave their credit cards at home when going to one of the super fishing stores because they can fill up a cart with hundreds of dollars of equipment without realizing it. You have to have some discipline not to buy everything that looks like it might catch a fish.

Quality fishing equipment is not cheap and the high-end equipment can cost a huge amount. With equipment like rods and reels it's best to buy good basic equipment that will hold up under use, but you shouldn't try to buy the top-of-the line equipment to get started. Buying equipment to use, not to show off and try to impress other fishermen, will save you money.

ALERT!

When you get to the level of fishing that requires a boat you can go into debt over your head. Bass boats can easily cost over $35,000 and the cheapest offshore fishing boats will run you much more. In the beginning, find someone to share a boat, or rent one to find out if you really want and need a boat.

Realistic Costs of Fishing

A good ultralight rod and reel can be purchased for less than $30. A freshwater combination rod and reel can be bought for less than $50. A basic saltwater outfit will be priced in the same range and often you can use the same equipment in both salt and fresh water. Add a few dollars for a spool of line, some terminal tackle and basic lures, and you can start fishing for $100 or less.

On the other extreme, the most expensive freshwater reels go for $450 to $550, and saltwater reels can cost much more. Add a custom rod for $500 and you break the $1,000 mark before you put on any line. However, most people never own such high-priced equipment no matter how fanatical they get.

A pack of hooks may cost less than a dollar but some specialty hooks run close to a dollar each. Many lures can be bought for a couple of dollars but some cost up to $20. Line runs from a few dollars for a bulk spool of 1,000 yards of some no-name brand to over $20 for 100 yards of a quality brand.

Start slowly, buy some basic equipment in the beginning, and add to it as your experience and tastes develop. Don't try to break the bank to get everything at once. Use some common sense and build your inventory gradually over time. You'll be surprised how quickly fishing equipment and tackle accumulates and you run out of space for it.

Bonding with Other Fishermen

Camaraderie among fishermen is legendary. If you spend a lot of time fishing with the same people, you develop a bond that is hard to break. From children fishing with parents and grandparents to best friends sharing a boat, fishing makes strong relationships.

Everyone wants to belong to a group and large numbers of fishing clubs have been formed to fill this need. From bass clubs that hold tournaments every month to carp clubs that stock and fish their own waters, clubs can be found to meet every fishing desire. And you can have a lot of fun while making friends and filling this basic human need.

FACT

There are more than 2,800 bass fishing clubs affiliated with the Bass Anglers Sportsman Society. Membership in those clubs totals about 50,000 fishermen in six countries and most states in the United States, with numbers growing.

Consider joining a club. You can learn from others in it, share expenses, and make lifetime friends. Or find a fishing partner if clubs don't appeal. Even a pair of fishermen has twice as much brainpower to figure out how to catch a fish.

Chapter 2

Choosing a Fish

There are tremendous numbers of fish swimming in the waters of our planet, and most of them can be caught while fishing. Deciding on which ones of them to pursue can be a confusing task, because there are a lot of choices to make. You have to decide if you want to fish fresh water or salt water, and for something to eat or just for the fun of it.

Where Do You Live?

If you live near the coast you have a choice between saltwater and freshwater fish. Saltwater fishing is not a good option if you live more than a couple of hours from the sea. You can't get to the fishing quickly enough to be able to go as often as you'll want to go. It's very frustrating to want to go fishing and not have enough time to get to the water you want to fish.

FACT

The International Game Fish Association Record Book lists records for over 800 species of fish that can be caught on rod and reel. They have line class records on the most popular of those fish, and that list includes 89 freshwater and 103 saltwater species.

People living in the deep south of the United States will never go ice fishing near home, nor will they catch many northern pike, either. Every continent has its own species of fish even though some have been transplanted worldwide. The area you live in will control the types of fish you can catch without a lot of traveling. It makes no sense to learn all you can about peacock bass if none live in the waters near you and you have to travel far from home to fish for them.

Watch your local paper for fishing reports and pictures of fish caught locally. Visit bait and tackle stores and talk to the people there to find out what common species are available near you. Visit local lakes and rivers and watch the fishermen. Talk to them in the parking lot at boat ramps and ask if they caught anything. They'll likely show you their catch and be glad to discuss it with you.

ALERT!

Don't be too pushy when talking to fishermen, and take everything they tell you with a grain of salt. You'll probably get accurate information about what was caught, but fishermen often consider what they used and where they caught them as "secret" info and won't tell you the truth.

Fishing Near Home

Fishing near home is easier in many ways. You can get there fast and spend more time fishing than traveling. If there's a problem, you're close to home and can get back quickly. Falling in the water on a cold day is no fun but is much better when you're only a few minutes from a hot shower and a change of clothes.

Expenses are much lower when you fish near home. Eating at home rather than on the road is cheaper, and if you travel any distance you'll have to find a place to sleep. You're more familiar with the area and can find cheaper gas and food when you need to purchase it, too.

Keeping fish is much more simple when you're near home. You can take the fish to a convenient place to clean them and then put the meat in the refrigerator or freezer. You have all the equipment you need at home to cook them in complicated recipes. Frying fish at home is much easier than it is on the road or while camping.

Traveling to Fish

Traveling to distant waters to fish can be a lot of fun. You can fish for different species that are new to you. You also get to see new scenery and experience different areas of the country. Even a drive of a few hours will often get you to totally different kinds of waters to fish

It is more expensive to travel and fish, but you can do things to keep expenses down. Camping is a great way to stay near the fish and lower your lodging and food costs if you plan to stay overnight. You can also put out set hooks and check them during the night. Sharing expenses with others is also a good way to cut costs.

But keeping fish can be a problem if you travel very far. If your trip is just a day or two, you can put the fish on ice and keep them cold until you get home and then clean them. Otherwise you need to clean the fish and keep the fillets or meat very cold until you get home. Cooking them while traveling is more difficult, too, since you need to carry all the cooking equipment with you. Grilling is the way to go when camping.

Fishing for Fun

Often called sport fishing, fishing for fun means you're going fishing to enjoy the challenge of catching the fish and the fight it gives you. You may keep some to eat but that is incidental to the fun of catching them. Most of the fish you catch will be released to fight another day. You may also target fish that aren't considered table fare, like muskie.

Sport fishing is done with rod and reel, and artificial lures are used most often. Sport fishermen can use live bait but some frown on using it. They say live bait takes the challenge out of catching the fish and makes fishing too easy. If the fight it more important than the effort to get the fish to bite, don't hesitate to use live bait. And some species like catfish require live or prepared bait since they don't take artificial bait as readily as other fish do.

Trying to set a line class record is definitely sport fishing. When trying to get your name in the record books you use the lightest line possible to catch the biggest fish around. Sometimes this effort goes to extremes that are dangerous to the fish, since long, hard fights can weaken them, and it also result in frustration to the angler when a big fish is lost. But it's a challenge and the reward of seeing your name in the record book is a thrill.

FACT

The International Game Fish Association has a special group of "clubs" of fishermen. The 20-to-1 club is for fishermen catching fish twenty times as heavy as the line test (the most weight a particular line will take before breaking). For example, you would have to catch a 200-pound fish on 10-pound line to qualify. There are also 15-to-1, 10-to-1 and 5-to-1 clubs.

Start Easy

Don't decide to start with the most challenging fish or try to set a record. You'll just disappoint yourself. Pick a game fish that's easy to catch and gradually work up to bigger and more challenging quarry. Beginners' luck sometimes seems to come into play and novices sometimes catch huge fish, but the catch makes news and is considered luck because it's an exception, not the rule.

If you're fishing in fresh water you should start with bream as your first fish. They're plentiful, easy to catch, and put up a good fight on light tackle. You can catch them on simple equipment and start enjoying the thrill of catching as well as the sport of fishing. You can also learn a lot by fishing for bream and watching how they behave, what happens when they bite, and how to unhook them. Carp and perch are other freshwater fish that share the same characteristics as bream and they can all be caught from the bank.

Saltwater fish that can be easy to catch for sport include topsail cats, drum, flounder, and pollock. They can all be caught from the bank and fight well on light tackle, so you don't need special equipment. Most of these fish hit live or prepared bait better than they do artificial baits, making them a little easier to catch. You can also learn about the way fish hit by fishing with live bait first. Fish are more likely to hit a live bait hard and come back more than once if you miss hooking them. Pay attention to the way they hit it and you'll be a better artificial bait fisherman, too.

Avoid Glamour Fish

Some fish such as freshwater bass get a lot of publicity, and there's a lot of hype about them in advertising. Many of the fishing television shows are about trying to catch bass. Fishermen spend millions of dollars trying to find the magic lure that will catch them. There are thousands of "weekend warriors" that fish club and local tournaments trying to catch them.

Bass can be extremely frustrating to catch, even for experienced anglers. In Georgia, bass clubs turn in a creel census report after each tournament. Over a twenty-year period the results are amazingly consistent. It takes bass club fishermen an average of five hours to catch one bass weighing an average of 1.6 pounds. Bass club fishermen are experienced bass fishermen for the most part. If it takes them that long to catch bass, it can be very frustrating to you when starting out.

Muskie are another fish that get a lot of space in fishing magazines. They're great to catch but a real challenge. Called the fish of 10,000 casts, they get that name from the difficulty of getting them to hit. Muskie fishermen say it takes an average of 10,000 casts to get one fish.

They are another fish that will frustrate you starting out.

Bonefish are a good example of a saltwater fish that's a real challenge to catch. They fight extremely well but have to be stalked, and casts to them have to be very accurate. Unless you hire a guide, bonefish are very hard to catch even for experienced fishermen. Wait until you have some experience catching fish before going after fish like these that are difficult to catch.

Fishing for Food

If your goal is to catch fish to eat, you'll probably go about it differently than if you were fishing for the thrill of the fight. There are many efficient ways to catch fish that don't even involve the use of rod and reel. You'll probably target the best-tasting fish rather than the strongest fighting ones, too.

Saltwater fish generally taste better than freshwater fish but are often harder to get to. If you want to catch dolphin, called mahi-mahi in restaurants, you'll need a boat. Others like flounder come close to shore and can be caught from beaches, piers, and bridges. Pick a fish that you have access to, rather than one that will cost you a lot of money to catch. Surf fishing on beaches is a good way to catch a variety of fish, as is pier fishing. A pier will get you out to deeper water where bigger fish live. Some piers are free while some charge a small amount to enter to fish. Many have bait and tackle shops on them so it's easy to get what you need. Fishing jetties can be good but be careful because waves breaking on the rocks can be dangerous.

When fishing for food, take along an ice chest. Kill the fish quickly by either hitting it with a "fish billy" or cutting it so it bleeds. Put it on ice as soon as you kill it. This will keep the fish as fresh as possible and they will have the best flavor.

Most freshwater fish can be caught from the bank but some are easier to catch than others. You can often cast to most of the water from the bank at a pond or stream, but big lakes and rivers have a lot of inaccessible water unless you have a boat. Some fish, such as bluegill, stay around the shoreline most of the time while others, like lake trout, are deep-water fish that can be caught only by trolling (trailing a line behind a slow-moving boat) or jigging (fishing with a device that you jerk up and down in the water) in very deep water. Consider those factors when choosing a fish, too.

Easy Food Fish

Many of the same fish that are easy to catch for sport also make good meals. Bream, perch, flounder, and pollock are all excellent when cooked. They fight well so you get the best of both parts of fishing. Other freshwater fish that are easy to catch and taste good are crappie and catfish. Crappie are some of the best freshwater fish around with sweet white flesh. They readily take minnows around shoreline brush in the spring and under bridges at night. Catfish hit bait fished on the bottom and can be caught from the bank in most lakes and rivers. Night fishing for them is excellent, too.

Some other saltwater fish that are easy to catch and taste good include croaker and sea bass. They can be caught off beaches, piers, and jetties and will put up a good fight, but are even better when cooked. Try for them to learn how to catch bigger, less aggressive saltwater fish.

Game Fish

Game fish are sought after for their fighting abilities. Smallmouth bass in fresh water, snook in coastal waters, and sailfish offshore are good examples of game fish. These fish will fight hard when hooked and give you a thrill while fighting them. They are a challenge to land when hooked.

FACT

Any fish that can be caught on rod and reel is considered a game fish by record-keeping organizations, but everyday fishermen don't see them that way. Game fish are considered the ones most desirable to catch and the ones you are most likely to brag about.

Most game fish are normally released so fishermen can enjoy their fight again. They're handled carefully and unhooked as gently as possible. You may be ostracized if you keep them to eat or even to mount as a trophy. When choosing a fish to pursue, remember this point if the opinion of other fishermen makes a difference to you.

Trash Fish

Some fishermen consider certain kinds of fish undesirable and call them trash, or junk, fish. These are usually fish that are not normally eaten and this designation goes back to when all fish were considered food fish. Other fishermen realize that all fish have some good qualities and go after them. Some fish that are considered trash fish, like gar in fresh water, put up an excellent fight. In salt water, some of the so-called trash fish are actually okay to eat and fishermen target them when more desirable species are not available.

Carp are considered trash fish in most of the United States but are sought after as game fish in many other countries. They're plentiful, they fight hard, and they can be eaten, although they have a lot of small bones. Consider targeting carp and have a lot of fun.

If you enjoy catching a fish or think it tastes good, don't worry too much about what others think. Go out and catch it, have fun, and eat a good meal. If someone asks about catching trash fish, just smile and tell that person you agree and he or she shouldn't try to catch them. Keep them to yourself.

Freshwater Fish

Freshwater fish are available to almost everyone close to home and offer a variety of types that fill every skill level and pocketbook. Many are excellent table fare and can be prepared in a variety of ways. You can catch them from the bank or from a boat, and boating for them is usually much easier than in salt water.

Common Freshwater Fish

Some freshwater fish like bass and bluegill are widespread, others like cutthroat trout and sturgeon have a limited range. Learning to catch one of the more widespread species makes traveling to new areas and catching fish easier. It's always challenging to try to learn to catch a new species, though, and some people keep a list of all the fish they have caught. You can enjoy reliving the catch of the ones on your list and the anticipation of adding new ones.

Ten popular freshwater fish are:

1. **Bass:** Black bass species include largemouth, smallmouth and spotted They're widespread and very popular.
2. **Bream:** Bluegill, shellcracker, pumpkinseed and many others make up this group of sunfish. They're easy to catch and some can be found in all fresh water.
3. **Carp:** Considered a trash fish by some, carp are a primary game fish in many countries. They grow big and fight hard.
4. **Catfish:** Flatheads, blue, and channel are the most popular catfish. They get huge, are found in most waters, and are very good to eat.
5. **Crappie:** One of the best fish to eat in fresh water. They can be found all across the United States and are not fished too often.
6. **Muskie:** A challenging fish to catch, muskie attract dedicated anglers who fish for nothing else. They're cool-water fish that grow to huge sizes.
7. **Pike:** A good fighting fish that is also fairly good to eat. Pike are usually found in cooler northern waters.
8. **Salmon:** Most salmon are spawned in fresh water and grow up in the sea, but some are landlocked. They fight well and are excellent table fare.
9. **Trout:** There are a wide variety of trout and they inhabit small streams to big lakes that stay cool year round. They're fun to catch and taste very good.

10. **Walleye:** According to many fishermen walleye are the best-tasting freshwater fish. They're a cool-water fish found in lakes and bigger streams and rivers.

These freshwater fish are all popular because they put up a good fight when hooked or are very good to eat. They're fairly widespread in the United States and most fishermen can fish for several of these species close to home. Some are easy to catch, others more of a challenge.

Advantages of Freshwater Fish

Accessibility to almost every fisherman is a big advantage of freshwater fish, because fresh water is almost always nearby. Plus, there are enough different kinds of freshwater fish to fulfill most any kind of fishing desire, and you seldom need special equipment to take them. Many kinds of freshwater fish can be landed on the most simple of equipment, and the water they live in won't corrode it nearly as bad as salt water does.

Disadvantages of Freshwater Fish

You'll need a state fishing license for all freshwater fishing in the United States and most other countries. There are strict number limits on most species and many have size limits, too. They don't taste as good as saltwater fish, and you usually can't catch as many fish as fast as you do in salt water.

Saltwater Fish

Saltwater fish inhabit all kinds of costal and open ocean water. They're very plentiful and many are excellent table fare. They can challenge you and your equipment when you hook one, because they're strong fighters, and some species grow to huge sizes.

Ten popular saltwater fish are:

1. **Barracuda:** A big toothy saltwater fish that puts up a strong fight when hooked.

2. **Bluefish:** Schooling blues can hit anything thrown at them and are easy to catch and good to eat.
3. **Bonefish:** A shallow-water flats fish known for its fast, long runs when hooked.
4. **Cod:** A bottom-dwelling fish that is excellent to eat.
5. **Croaker:** An inshore bottom-feeding fish that is very good to eat.
6. **Drum:** A bottom-feeding fish that puts up a strong fight and is good to eat.
7. **Flounder:** These flatfish lie on the bottom and have both eyes on one side of their head. They're very good to eat.
8. **Shark:** A wide variety of sharks inhabit salt water and all fight hard.
9. **Snapper:** An excellent food fish that lives in warmer waters.
10. **Striped Bass:** These hard-fighting fish spawn in freshwater rivers and live in salt water.

These saltwater fish are widespread and you can find some of them in most areas. Watch for information about these fish near where you live and check at the docks when boats come in to see if they've caught any of them.

Advantages of Saltwater Fish

If you live near the coast you have access to a wide variety of fish. They outnumber their freshwater cousins in species as well as individual fish. Fish in salt water usually feed more voraciously so they're often easier to catch. And you can fish for them in a wide variety of ways, from putting a bait out on the bottom to trolling offshore. Many people are willing to travel long distances to enjoy fishing for saltwater fish.

Disadvantages of Saltwater Fish

Some kinds of saltwater fish are hard to get to without spending a lot of money. If you don't live near the coast you have to travel long distances to get to them, and some species don't come in close to shore so you have to go out in a boat. The sea can get very dangerous so you must have a boat that can handle it. And many saltwater fish have teeth that make handling them more difficult. When fishing salt water you're not at the top of the food chain!

ALERT!

Be even more careful when handling saltwater fish than you are with freshwater fish. Never put your fingers in the mouth of a saltwater fish without carefully checking first. Almost all saltwater fish have teeth or bony plates in their mouths that will hurt you.

Big-Game Fish

Unless you just won the lottery you probably won't start your fishing experience with big-game fish. Even if you go out on a charter boat, the cheapest way to fish for marlin, sailfish, swordfish, tuna, and other huge saltwater fish, it will cost you at least $600 a day. Some people get a taste of big-game fishing by chartering a boat while on vacation. Although it's expensive, you get a full day on the water and the experience of fishing for these kinds of fish. If you're already in an area where charters are available, consider it. You might even be able to find another fisherman or two to join you and split the costs. Ⓔ

Chapter 3
Ways to Fish

Different kinds of waters and different species of fish require different methods and tackle to get your bait to them. Some methods and tackle are appropriate over a wide range of conditions and some are very specialized. You can choose a way to fish that is active and requires a lot of effort or a method that lets the bait work while you relax.

Pole and Line

A hand line is the most simple of tackle but has limited use. It was probably the earliest method of fishing with a hook and line. Adding a pole gives you more leverage when you hook fish and helps you land them. And it's usually more fun fighting a fish on a pole and line than just on a line by itself.

Equipment Needed for Pole and Line Fishing

Poles now range from traditional cane poles to modern fiberglass poles that retract into themselves for easy transport. They can be any length but fourteen to sixteen feet is about average. Shorter poles are easier to handle but limit your reach. With longer poles you can get your bait out farther away from you.

Lines are attached to the tip of the pole and should be about as long as the pole. Any kind of line can be used but monofilament is the traditional line to use on a pole. Add a hook and you're ready to fish. Most people also use a small cork or float and a Split Shot (a kind of sinker) above the hook to hold the bait in place. Bait at the end of the line can vary from earthworms to artificial baits, depending on how and where you're fishing, and what you're trying to catch.

When starting out, and especially for kids, tie line to the pole that is a few feet shorter than the pole is long. That makes it much harder to hook yourself when holding the end of the pole.

How to Use a Pole and Line

Basically, tie a line to the end of the pole, put a cork, Split Shot, and hook on the end of the line, bait up with a worm, and drop it into the water. That's it! Bream, catfish, bass, and many other kinds of freshwater fish will hit a worm suspended under a cork. A saltwater variation is to put a gob of worms on a hook without weight or float and drop it around the edge of marsh grass for mullet.

After baiting up you raise the pole tip while holding the bait in your other hand. As the tip of the pole rises, release the bait and swing it out over the water. Drop the tip of the pole when the bait gets to the right spot to drop it into the water. With practice you can place the bait right where you want it and not make a splash as it enters the water. You can learn to drop it right beside a bush or stump for exact placement, which is sometimes needed.

When holding the bait before swinging it out over the water, be very careful of the hook. It's best to hold the line a few inches above the bait and hook so the point of the hook won't stick you when you release it.

When a fish hits, you simply raise the pole, setting the hook and pulling the fish toward the surface. You bring the fish out of the water and to you with a pendulum motion if the fish is small enough, or, if the fish is too big, work it toward you by raising the pole tip to lift it out of the water. Walking away from the water will work if you are fishing from the bank. Or pulling in the pole hand over hand to get to the line after fighting the fish will work if you're in a boat. You can quickly take the fish off and put new bait on the hook and be back in the water waiting on the next bite.

Fishing with pole and line is very efficient and can be learned quickly. Costs are low and the equipment is simple. It's a good method to use to learn to fish.

You can buy a cane pole with line, hook, sinker, and float, and a cup of earthworms for bait, for less than $10. It's by far the cheapest way to get started fishing and there's very little to break on a cane pole.

When to Use a Pole and Line

Choose a pole and line any time you can get close to the fish. It's hard to fish more than twenty-five feet away with a pole and line. You also need to be close to the water, so fishing from high piers with pole and line is difficult. It's excellent when you need to drop your bait into an exact spot close to you without making a splash. This method is also best with live or prepared bait.

Fishing from the bank of a pond or stream for bream and catfish is the traditional use for pole and line. Easing along the bank of a lake, dropping a live minnow or jig beside the brush to catch crappie in the spring is a ritual with pole and line in the South. Catching mullet on poles is also a traditional method in salt water. It's best to fish with pole and line in relatively shallow water, because fishing deeper than the length of the pole is difficult.

Skitterpoling is an old method of catching bass, pike, and other cover-loving fish. A strong two-foot piece of line is attached to the tip of a long, heavy pole, and a lure that makes a lot of surface noise is tied to it. This bait is skittered along the top of the water near cover until a fish hits.

Poles and lines don't get along well with overhanging tree limbs. You need a clear area with enough room over your head and over the water to raise and swing the pole. You can drop the bait under overhanging brush but it must be far enough away from you to give you room to move the pole.

Casting

Casting is probably the method of fishing visualized by most people when thinking about fishing. Casting is a method of throwing the bait and using its weight to get it where you want it. There are many ways to cast, making it the most versatile way to fish. You can catch just about any fish that swims by casting and you can also fish in almost any kind of waters you encounter.

Equipment Needed for Casting

A rod-and-reel combination is needed for casting. You can use any kind of outfit but you need a reel that will hold the line and allow it to play out when you cast the bait. The type of rod can vary a lot, too, but it must be capable of holding the reel and having a way to guide the line to the tip of the rod that will allow it to go out.

The basic kinds of reels used to cast the bait are spinning, casting, and spin-casting. Each works in a different way but all hold line and allow it to go out freely when cast. Rods can vary from short three-foot ultralight types that are very limber to stout surf rods eleven feet long and capable of throwing a weight that would break an ultralight. Most rods have guides wrapped with thread and glued on them to guide the line to the tip, but some have a method of running the line through the center of the rod to guide it.

FACT

Spinning reels hang under the rod. Bait-casting and spin-casting reels sit on top of the rod. Spinning rods have big guides that are placed under the rod; the other two have smaller guides that sit on top of the rod to line up with the reel.

Just about any kind of fishing line can be used in casting. Monofilament is the norm but specialized lines are available to fit any specific need. Depending on the type of cover you're fishing and the kind of fish you're after, you can pick a line that is best for that purpose.

Cost can vary from a few dollars for a basic spin-casting outfit to over $1,000 for a quality reel and custom-made rod. To start out, you don't need the most expensive equipment but you should buy outfits that will work consistently well and hold up under use. And the type you learn on will often be your favorite for a long time, since you get the basics of using it down first.

How to Use Casting Equipment

There are a lot of variations on casting but all require you to hold the line at the spool so it doesn't release until you want it to. You can release the line with your thumb, your finger, a trigger, or a push button, depending on the type of reel. You swing the rod tip to throw the lure or bait and release the line at the correct point in the rod swing. When the bait hits the water you turn a handle to engage the line and start reeling it in.

To cast, do the following depending on what kind of reel you're using:

- With a spin-casting reel, push the button in and hold it to keep the line from releasing.
- With a trigger reel, hold the trigger in to keep the line from releasing.
- With a spinning reel catch the line with your trigger finger and hold it to keep it from releasing while opening the bail.
- With a bait-casting reel, hold your thumb against the spool to keep the line from releasing and push the free spool button.
- With all three kinds of reels, hold the line as you make the cast, releasing it to spool out at the correct point in the cast.

Casting each kind of reel takes a slightly different action by your hands and you must get used to each kind. Once you master one, it's easier to switch to one of the other kinds since the casting motion is the same. The release of the line is what's different.

FIGURE 3-1

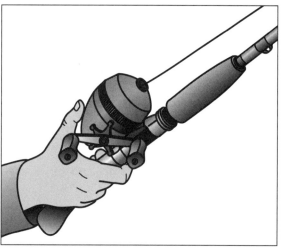

◄ Thumbing a spin-casting reel.

FIGURE 3-2

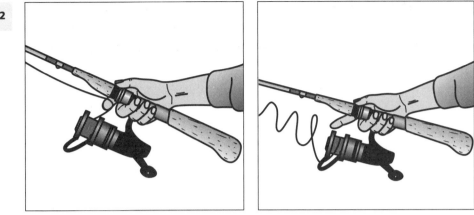

▲ A line release on a spinning reel.

FIGURE 3-3

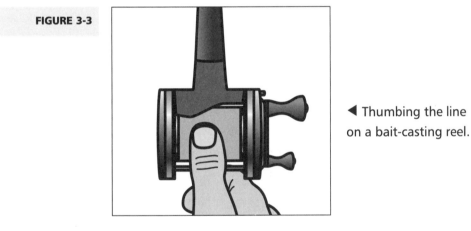

◀ Thumbing the line on a bait-casting reel.

Learning to cast takes practice, no matter what kind of outfit you use. A few minutes in the backyard or on the water with a practice plug can save you trouble later when you want to catch a fish. Start off without hooks for both safety's sake and to keep your line from snagging onto things. You must coordinate the action of your hand moving the rod with the action of your fingers or thumb releasing the line at the correct time. It's easier than it sounds and most kids older than six pick it up quickly.

To cast you:

1. Hold the line at the reel.
2. Face your target and point the rod tip at it.
3. Flex your elbow to raise the rod tip over your head.
4. With a smooth, continuous motion, whip the rod tip back toward the target.
5. Release the line at the reel when the rod tip is at about a forty-five-degree angle.
6. Follow through with the rod tip until it's pointed at the target again.

FIGURE 3-4

▲ The casting motion with a bait-casting outfit.

When to Use Casting Equipment

Casting works for almost all fishing situations for getting the bait to the fish. You can throw a surf bait well over 100 feet with the right equipment, or you can pitch a plastic worm to a tree trunk ten feet away. Casting works from the bank, from a boat, and from piers and jetties. And you can cast baits as light as a feather or as heavy as a hammer with the right outfit.

To set the free spool on bait-casting reels, tie a lure on the line and hold it at the rod tip at a forty-five-degree angle in front of you. Push the free spool button and adjust the tension so the lure descends to the floor and the spool stops spinning when it hits the floor.

You can learn to cast a bait so that it enters the water without making a ripple (for easily spooked fish) or you can let it splash down (to draw the attention of schooling fish). Casting to shoreline cover while bass fishing, throwing a bait a long way when surf fishing, or casting to grass beds while trying to get a muskie are all good ways to use casting equipment.

Fly-Fishing

Fly-fishing is different in that you cast the *line,* not the lure. This allows you to throw extremely light flies that can't be presented in any other way. Fly-fishing is efficient because you can make a lot of casts quickly so the bait doesn't stay in one place very long (just like a real fly). Fish also put up a great fight on fly rods because the rods tend to be light and limber.

Equipment Needed for Fly-Fishing

Reels don't have to be complex because all they do is hold the line. For trout and other freshwater fish, most of the fighting of the fish is done by pulling in line with your hands so the reel is not important there, either. Some reels have handles you crank to retrieve line, others have a lever that activates a spring to wind in the line. Reels for big salt- and freshwater fish that make long runs, like salmon and steelhead, do have a drag system to help you fight the fish.

The rod is the most important part of fly-fishing because it is what's used to throw the line. Rods are long and limber, often eight to ten feet in length. Fly line is thick and heavy enough to be cast; some kinds float and others sink. A monofilament leader is attached to the end of the line to separate the bait from the thick fly line that might spook a fish.

How to Use Fly-Fishing Equipment

Some people say fly-fishing is standing in the water waving a stick. But most fly-fishing is done away from the shoreline while wading or from a boat because the motion you use makes the line go almost as far behind you as it does in front of you.

For fly-fishing, pull enough line off the reel and through the guides so several feet lay in the water in front of you. Start waving the rod tip back and forth to get the line moving in the air. Strip more line off at the reel and release it on the forward cast to add more length to the cast. Continue this motion until enough line is out to reach your target.

Watch out for anything behind you on your back cast. You don't want to hit trees, bushes, or other people. Be very aware that your line goes out as far behind you as it does in front of you.

Remember, you must keep the line moving. Wait on the back cast until you feel it get tight before starting your forward motion. Start with a short line out and learn to cast just twenty feet or so, then gradually work up to longer distances.

FIGURE 3-5 A

FIGURE 3-5 B

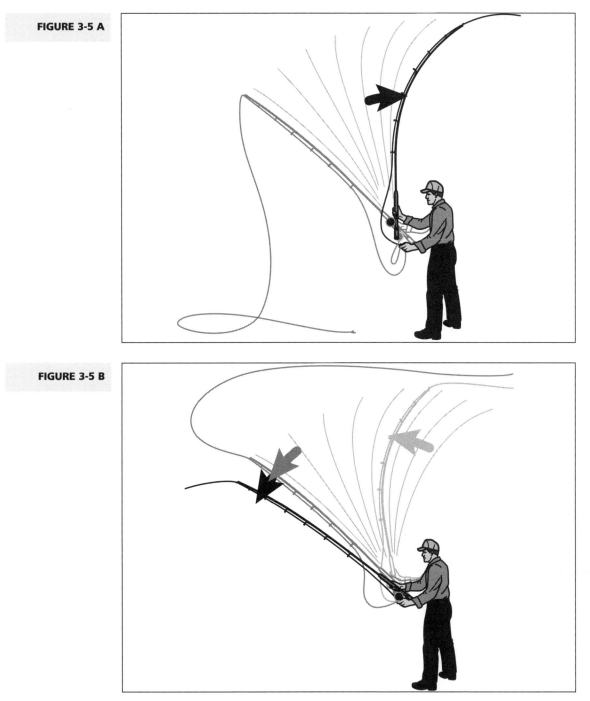

▲ Casting with a fly rod.

When to Use Fly-Fishing Equipment

The traditional use of a fly rod is fishing for trout using tiny feather lures. But you can use a fly rod any time and just about any place. From throwing small popping bugs for bream to throwing huge streamers for tarpon, you can catch any size fish in any kind of water. Pick a fly rod if you want to accentuate the fight of a fish. If you want to quickly drop a lure into an area, then move it to the next one, use a fly rod. Since you don't have to reel in between cast, you can quickly drop your bait, move it a little to attract a fish, then cast to the next spot. It's a very efficient way to catch fish.

Trolling

Trolling means pulling your lure or bait behind the boat as it moves along. You can troll with any kind of equipment from hand lines to fly rods but casting equipment is the norm in fresh water. In salt water, special short, heavy rods with huge reels designed to hold a lot of line and fight monster game fish are used for trolling.

FACT

Trolling is illegal in some states. Check local regulations for details. In some places you can troll while paddling but not while using any kind of motor; in others it's illegal to troll under any circumstances.

You must have a boat to troll. Find a suitable area where you want to fish and start moving slowly over it in your boat. Tie on a lure or bait and drop it into the water. Slowly let out line until it's far enough behind the boat and working deep enough to attract fish. You can vary your speed to entice the fish. Trolling is much easier on boats with electric or gas motors than it is on ones you have to paddle yourself.

Drift-Fishing

Drift-fishing is similar to trolling but you let the wind or current move your lure or bait. It can be done from a boat or from the bank of a river or stream with current, and you can use the tides in salt water to drift your bait. This method allows your bait to move naturally with the current or the wind and is more quiet than trolling since no motors or paddles are involved. Check local regulations since drift-fishing from a boat is sometimes illegal.

From a boat, get into position so the wind or current will take you across the area you want to fish. Drop your lure or bait down and let it drag as you move. You can drift very slowly and keep your bait right under the boat or let out line and drag it behind the boat. A cork or bobber on the line will keep the bait near the surface or you can let it down to fish any depth between the surface and bottom.

From the shore of a river or stream, cast out and then let the current move your bait. A float works well for this kind of drift-fishing. You cast upstream and let the current move your bait, suspended under the float, downstream. You can either sit still or move down the bank with your bait if there's room.

When fishing the beach, if you can find a current running down the beach, or during an outgoing tide, you can let those currents move your bait. Since these currents are usually slow you'll probably need to use some kind of float.

Still-Fishing

Still-fishing is a method of letting the bait sit in one place and waiting for a passing fish to bite. You can use any kind of tackle. Put your rod in a holder or even prop it in a forked limb; then sit back and watch your line for a bite. With set hooks you can do something else and come back later to check them.

Catfish are traditionally still-fished, but other species will hit using this method, including saltwater fish. Surf-fishing, where you put your rod in a sand spike (a type of holder), is a form of still-fishing. You can even still-fish with a rod and reel by casting out a bait and letting it sit, usually on the bottom. Use a lead weight heavy enough to keep the bait there; don't use a float, because the bait will drift out of position.

Many people like to find a suitable place on the bank where they can cast to deep water and put out several rods in holders. They build a fire and sit back to wait on a bite. This is a very relaxing way to fish and you can catch a lot of fish using this method. Still-fishing can be done at night or during the day.

Other people set out limb lines, which are short lengths of line with a hook tied to one end and tied to limbs overhanging the water. The lines are long enough for the bait to reach the water and a sinker is sometimes used to hold the bait down, especially in rivers with current.

Another method of still-fishing is setting up a trotline, which is a long line tied horizontally between two places, often two trees on the bank or on either side of a cove or creek. Short dropper lines with hooks on them are tied to the long line and spaced along it. Trotlines can cover a lot of different water depths and you can bait up the dropper lines with different baits. Trotlines often have twenty-five to fifty hooks on them.

Jug fishing is another type of still-fishing. A short dropper line is tied to a jug and baited up. The jug is thrown into the water to drift around, presenting the bait to fish in different areas. You'll need a boat to retrieve the jugs and fish on them. Many people put jugs out just before dark and retrieve them at daylight the next morning.

Wading

Wading is a good way to get to fish in shallow water and can be the best way to fish for some species, like trout, in streams. But you must be careful. Getting into the water adds some danger to fishing, from slipping and hurting yourself to dropping tackle and losing it. But it's worthwhile if you're careful.

In warm water you can wade in shorts and tennis shoes but cold water requires waders (waterproof pants with boots attached) that will keep you dry and warm. Walk carefully and fish going upstream, casting to places holding fish ahead of you. That way you won't spook them by stirring up mud and debris that will float over them. In still waters walk carefully and slowly or you'll scare the fish.

Hip waders come up to your hip and chest waders come to your chest. Both are held up with straps and keep you dry while wading in cold water. You can wear insulated pants under them for even more warmth.

A long stick is often used to help brace yourself while you wade. You can fish with any kind of rod and reel, but a fly rod is traditional. And wading gives you room for your back cast when using a fly rod. Give wading a try if there are suitable waters near you, but be careful. (E)

Chapter 4

Choosing a Rod

If you walk into a discount store and go to the tackle section, you'll find a forest of rods sticking up above the counter. They will range from short, limber rods to very long, heavy rods. Some will have small guides (the devices that feed the line to the tip) the length of the rod but others will have much bigger guides near the handle. Picking the right rod can be a bewildering experience.

Fiberglass or Graphite?

Most modern rods are made of fiberglass, graphite, or a combination of the two. They've been used for many years, although fiberglass has been around longer. Both make good rods and each has qualities that make rods different. Graphite rods usually cost more than a fiberglass rod of the same quality, but a good fiberglass rod will be a lot more expensive than a cheap graphite rod.

How Rods Are Made

Rods are made by wrapping a very thin sheet of long fibers of graphite or fiberglass material around a tapered dowel. These fibers run the length of the rod and the sheet is held together by glue. It takes several layers of the sheets of fiber to make the rod. When enough have been wrapped, the whole rod is finished with a coating to make it smooth. When the dowel is removed the rod is hollow and the finished product is called a rod blank.

The stiffer the fibers the stiffer the rod will be, and using more fibers makes a strong rod, but also means it's heavier. Graphite is stiffer and lighter than fiberglass so it makes a stiff, light rod, but graphite rods are also more brittle than fiberglass rods. The higher-quality rods are made of a very stiff, thin wall of fibers, meaning they're light and sensitive, but they're also brittle and more likely to break. As with most things, picking a rod is a compromise among several factors.

ALERT!

Because of the way rods are made, a sharp blow or rap to them can cause a hidden fracture that will fail later. This is often a problem when in a boat, because it's easy to hit the side of the boat when casting. Even dropping the rod can damage it, so avoid hitting your rod against anything.

Guides are placed on the rod blank and wrapped with thread. This thread is then covered with an epoxy to hold it and protect it. Placement and type of guides is very important. The guides must line up with each other to allow line to flow through them freely. They must be big enough to allow the line to move easily through them. And guides must be hard enough to withstand the abrasion of the line moving across them.

A handle, which includes the reel seat, is placed on the rod. Handles are either straight or pistol grip on casting and spin-casting rods, and straight on spinning rods. The way the reel attaches to the rod varies, but it must be secure and solid enough so that the reel will not move. And the reel seat must line up with the bottom guide.

Rod Taper

Rod action or stiffness is determined by the type and amount of fiber used. Rods can be very stiff or very flexible for their full length, but all of them must have tips that are more flexible than the end near the reel. This is called *taper*. A fast-taper rod is stiff near the tip, a medium-taper rod flexes about halfway down, and a slow-taper rod flexes its full length. Each has its specific uses and performs better at certain kinds of fishing.

FIGURE 4-1

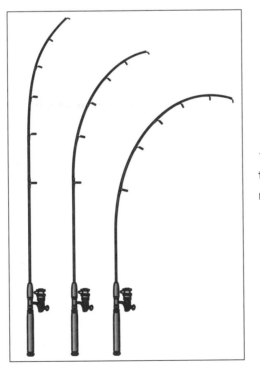

◀ From left to right: a fast-taper rod, a medium-taper rod, and a slow-taper rod.

When fishing a soft bait like liver, earthworms, and bloodworms, use a slow-taper rod. Casting with them is a softer action and they're less likely to tear the bait or throw it off. And when using live bait it's easier to hook the fish, lowering the need for a stiff rod.

A fast-taper rod is better for setting the hook hard when bass fishing, or trying to hook a hard-mouthed saltwater fish like a tarpon. It will not flex as much when fighting a fish, though, so those rods require a heavier line. Slow-taper rods are good for ultralight fishing since they flex more and don't put as much pressure on the line. It's much harder to get a good hook set with them, though. A medium rod tries to combine the best of both.

Rod Sensitivity

Sensitivity is the ability of the rod to transfer vibrations to your hands. This is important because it's one of the ways you can detect what's going on at the end of you line, and the way you feel the fish fight. Fast-action rods with stiff fibers are more sensitive than slow-taper rods. Graphite fibers are stiffer and therefore more sensitive than fiberglass. So for the best sensitivity, get a fast-taper graphite rod.

What can I tell by flexing a rod in the store?
Not much. To find out if you will like a rod, take it fishing or at least try casting it outside the store. Put a reel, line, and practice plug on the rod and try it out before buying it.

QUESTION?

Rod Length

Short rods are easier to transport and less likely to hit things when you're casting, and are best for fishing in confined places. Longer rods are better for throwing a bait a long way, setting the hook, and fighting strong fish. Short ultralight rods are usually made with a slower taper, and longer, heavier rods have a faster taper. Most casting rods range from five to seven feet in length. Some specialized rods like surf rods and flipping sticks are made longer and have other specific qualities for their purpose.

Choose a rod that is a convenient length to use where you fish. You don't want a seven-foot rod if you walk the bank of a river and cast where there are a lot of overhanging trees near your head. A seven-foot rod would be appropriate for fishing heavy jigs around offshore oil rigs.

Most rods are one or two piece but some rods made for traveling break down into several short lengths. As a rule of thumb, get a one-piece rod if you can transport it without problems. It will be more sensitive and you should have fewer problems with it. If you need a two-piece rod, make sure the ferrules (fittings) where the pieces join are tight and keep them coated with wax so they will come apart.

Ferrules are usually made from the same material as the blank, although a few are still made of metal. The fiberglass and graphite ferrules are a better match to the rod, because they give the rod a more consistent taper, and don't stick together as often as metal ones. Avoid metal ferrules if possible.

A Simple Pole

A pole is one of the simplest fishing tools. It can be made of cane, fiberglass, or graphite, and it comes in a wide variety of lengths and actions for various kinds of fishing. Many of the fiberglass and graphite models telescope into themselves to make transport easier. Some cane poles also break down into two or more pieces joined with a ferrule.

Pick a pole that is the right action and length for your fishing. An extremely light pole is good for panfish (that's a fish usually cooked whole) like bream and small cats. You'll need a heavier pole for crappie, bass, and bigger catfish. If you fish around saltwater jetties with a pole you will need a fairly heavy one for the stronger fish found there.

Choose a pole that is the right length, too. A longer pole gives you the ability to place your bait farther away, but it's also heavier and harder to handle. Pick one that you can easily hold up while waiting for a bite. If it is too long it will be tiring and you won't want to use it.

Spin-Casting Rods

Spin-casting rods have small guides on them and are usually fairly light since spin-cast reels work best with lighter line. They are generally shorter than other types of rods, too. The handle and guides line up and are arranged to be held with the reel and guides on top of the rod.

FIGURE 4-2

▲ A spin-casting rod with a pistol grip.

Spin-Casting Rod Quality

Spin-casting rods are often some of the cheapest made. They're usually considered beginners' equipment and a lot of them are more like toys for kids. They're sometimes made of one piece of fiberglass and don't have long fibers in them to make them stiff and strong. It is best to stay away from these cheap rods since they won't do a good job and will not hold up.

Look at the finish on a higher-quality spin-casting rod. Is it smooth and blemish free? Does it have a clear coat over it or is it uncoated fiberglass? If it has a ferrule, is it tight but comes apart easily? Is the rod straight if

you hold it up and look down the side opposite the line guides? If the answer to any of these questions is no, look at another rod.

The Reel Seat on a Spin-Casting Rod

The reel foot or reel seat is the flat metal or plastic piece on the reel that attaches to the rod. It is supported by a short stem on spinning rods but is attached to the side of bait-casting and casting reels. The guide foot is the part of the guide that attaches to the reel. Double-footed guides have a foot on each side of the guide and single-footed guides have just one. They are under the wrapping on the rods and out of sight after the rod is made.

Most spin-casting rods have a simple screw and foot to hold the reel in place. You slide one end of the reel foot into a slot and then place the other end under a foot. A screw going through the rod handle tightens down the foot on the reel seat to hold it tight. Keep some wax or grease on this screw so you'll be able to remove the reel if you need to take it off.

Handles on spin-casting rods can be either pistol grip or straight. The pistol grip helps you hold the rod better on the cast, but it's shorter than the straight grip, so you don't have the extra length for leverage when casting or fighting a fish. Handles may be made of plastic, cork, or other materials. Make sure they're textured so your hand won't slip, but smooth enough to hold comfortably.

Guides on a Spin-Casting Rod

Guides on a spin-casting rod should line up with each other when you look down the rod through them. They should be evenly spaced, and the more guides the better. They will probably be metal guides with no added insert in the eye, and most will have two feet, one on each side of the guide. You should run a cotton swab or piece of nylon cloth through the guide to make sure it's smooth. Any rough place will fray your line.

The wrapping on spin-casting rods may be a plastic tape or a kind of heat-shrink sleeve that holds it tight. Better rods will have guides wrapped with thread and then coated with epoxy. The coating over the guide feet should be smooth and slick with no bumps or nicks.

Spinning Rods

Spinning rods come in all lengths, tapers, and prices, and can be used for a wide range of fishing, some are very specialized. An average spinning rod is six to seven feet long but ultralight models can be much shorter, and those suitable for surf-fishing can be well over twelve feet long.

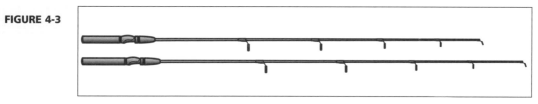

▲ Spinning rods.

Spinning Rod Quality

Spinning rods range from cheap toys to very expensive tournament tools. They can be made from solid fiberglass to the finest types of graphite. Guides range from simple metal rings to expensive ceramic guides that ensure line will not be damaged. The finish on them can be a smooth, shiny surface that will hold up for years or uncoated fiberglass.

Look for a rod that's straight when you hold it horizontal to the floor, with no curves or other flaws. It should be light enough to hold comfortably, and balanced so the tip is slightly heavier to offset the weight of the reel. The surface should be smooth and blemish free, and there should not be any rough places on it where the guides are attached.

The Reel Seat on a Spinning Rod

The reel seat on a spinning rod is important because you hold the rod at it and your fingers wrap around it. Many reel seats on spinning rods have a cushion on them to make it easier to hold for long periods of time. With or without a cushion, the reel seat should be smooth and have no edges or protrusions that will hurt your hand when holding it a long time.

Spinning reels can have the following types of reel seats.

- **Clamp and foot:** A lever lifts up to release a foot that holds the reel seat and clamps down to lock it in place.
- **Screw and foot:** A screw goes through the rod handle and tightens a foot on the other side to hold the reel seat.
- **Screw ring:** A ring is threaded around the handle and screws a foot to move it down a slot to grip the reel seat.
- **Sliding sleeve:** A sleeve around the rod slides down to clamp the reel seat in place.
- **Slip ring:** A sliding ring goes over each end of the reel seat and wedges it in place.
- **Tennessee handle:** No seat at all; you tape the reel to the rod handle.

All of these reel seats will do the job but the ones that have sleeves covering the reel foot will be easier on your hand. The more simple ones are less likely to cause problems and malfunction, and some are much heavier than others. Just make sure the one you choose moves freely and holds the reel securely in a straight line with the guides.

Guides on a Spinning Rod

Guides should be spaced evenly and the one nearest the reel handle should be very large. They should get progressively smaller to the tip. The guides should also be made with hard materials like titanium or have a ceramic insert in them. Look for information about the guides on the rod or on its tag.

FACT

Line comes off spinning reels in big loops and a bigger guide at the handle helps control the loop and feed it smoothly through the other guides. The first guide makes the loop smaller and the second guide tames it even more.

The wrap on spinning rod guides should be tight and smooth. The threads should be wrapped so tightly together that you need a magnifying glass to see the individual wraps. Guides may have a foot on each side or just one foot. With either kind there should be no space between the guide foot and the rod.

Bait-Casting Rods

Rods made for bait-casting reels are usually heavier, longer, and stronger. Casting reels can handle the heaviest line of any so the rods made for them range from fairly light to extremely strong and tough. And you can find them in any length and taper for your specific needs.

▲ A bait-casting rod.

Bait-Casting Rod Quality

A smooth blemish-free finish is a sign of a good bait-casting rod. The higher-quality rods have a deep glow to them from the finish applied to the rod blank. Look for a rod that is perfectly straight, has numerous guides on it, and is not tip heavy. A bait-casting rod should balance right at the reel seat because rods that are tip heavy will tire your hand.

The Bait-Casting Rod Reel Seat

The reel seat on a bait-casting rod must be very strong for heavier uses. It can be any arrangement that grips the reel foot and tightens down to hold it securely. Most are some kind of screw and foot arrangement because they tend to be the strongest. There should be no protrusions on it, to hurt your hand while fishing.

A popular type of handle in recent years is the through-handle. Rather than the rod attaching to the end of the handle, this type has the rod blank run all the way through it. Some even have cutouts exposing parts of the blank. Through-handles are supposed to transmit feel to your hand better than others. They can be found on all kinds of rods.

Never buy a rod until you put a reel on it and feel its balance and weight. When holding the rod with the reel on it, grasp it just like you would while fishing and make sure it's comfortable and you will be able to hold it for long periods of time.

Guides on a Bait-Casting Rod

Guides should be straight and in line with each other on bait-casting rods as with all other kinds of rods. They're not much bigger at the handle end of the rod since line comes off bait-casting reels in a straight line. The first guide needs to be big enough to handle the sideways movement as the line comes off the spool, but it doesn't have to be large like a spinning rod guide.

The thread wrapping bait-casting rods should be tight and smooth. There should not be any bumps or tag ends of line showing if they're wrapped correctly. No knots are used in wrapping a guide so you should see no evidence of one. The transition from rod surface to wrap surface should be smooth and not have a sharp edge to it.

Hard guides made of metal or those with ceramic inserts should be used to prevent damage to the line. If you plan on using a braid or other abrasive line, check the rod documentation for information about the guides. Make sure they can handle these types of lines.

Single-footed guides are also found on bait-casting rods. They're lighter and work just as well as double-footed guides. They should be solid and tight, without any movement. They should also be perfectly aligned with the rod blank. Check this since they're a little harder to line up when putting on the blank.

The more guides on a rod the better, up to a point. Quality rods may have a guide every six to eight inches to keep the line away from the blank when fighting a strong fish. If a six-foot rod has fewer than six guides you should consider another rod.

Fly Rods

You can buy a fiberglass, graphite, or bamboo fly rod. The bamboo rods are very expensive and are seldom used by any but the most discriminating fisherman. Fly rods are much longer than other types and have to be more flexible because they cast the line, not the lure. Fly line is very thick so guides can be simple wire loops to save weight.

FIGURE 4-5

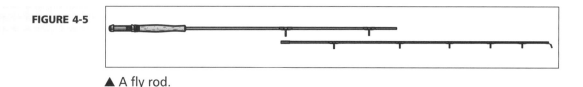

▲ A fly rod.

Fly Rod Quality

Fly rods run from inexpensive fiberglass rods suitable for beginners to split bamboo rods that are collector items. They must have a slick surface so line doesn't drag on them and should be light enough to handle for long periods of time without tiring you out. You will constantly wave a fly rod over your head while using it, so keep weight and balance in mind.

The Reel Seat on a Fly Rod

The reel seat on a fly rod attaches at the very end to help balance the weight of the rod. To cast, you grasp the rod in front of the reel seat and strip off line with your other hand. The reel seat is usually a simple collar around the rod that screws down to push a ring tight around the seat. Except on saltwater fly rods and those used for big, hard-fighting fish like steelhead, little pressure is put on the reel.

Guides on a Fly Rod

Guides on fly rods used for smaller fish aren't as important since you fight the fish with the rod and there is not much movement of line across the guides. Alignment should be straight and close enough together to keep sharp angles out of the line when fighting a fish with a bent rod. Wrap should be snag free and the thread should be coated with epoxy.

What Rods Cost

Rods can cost a few dollars or many hundreds of dollars. Picking one that does a good job for you without spending too much money is not hard if you spend some time looking at rods and learning about them. A basic rod costing less than $50 is suitable for many kinds of fishing and will serve you well. As you get more experienced and want specialized rods and higher quality rods, you may spend more.

ALERT!

Compare the cost of rods, because prices vary greatly for the same rod. It's a good idea to check prices online, in catalogs, and in the store before you buy a high-quality rod. Just make sure you're comparing the exact same rod in all places.

At some point in your fishing career you may decide to purchase a custom-made rod. Nothing is better because a good rod maker will find out exactly what you want and fill that desire. A good custom-made rod becomes an extension of your hand and will give you better a feel than others. Of course, this quality doesn't come cheap. It is not unusual to pay several hundred dollars for a basic custom rod for casting, and specialized rods cost even more. Consider a custom-made rod when you reach the time in your fishing that you want the best, and can afford it.

Chapter 5

Choosing a Reel

A reel can be as simple as a handle on a line-filled spool or as complicated as a delicate machine that spins as smooth as silk. They all have similarities, though. They all provide a place for the line to be stored, a method for storing the line until you want to release it, and a way to wind it back in. Most have some kind of drag system, too.

Spin-Casting Reels

A spin-casting reel is often the first one a new fisherman buys. Also called closed-face reels, they're simple to operate and often very inexpensive. Most are made to sit on top of the rod, but a few are designed to hang under it. You can buy a quality spin-casting reel that works well, but many of the cheaper ones often have problems and don't work as well as other kinds of reels.

FIGURE 5-1

◄ A spin-casting reel.

How a Spin-Casting Reel Works

A revolving cap sits over the spool of line inside the cover of the reel. A push button or a lever on the reel allows you to hold the line tight in the reel while making a cast. A pin in the side of the cap works in and out with the push button and handle of the reel. When you push the button the pin drops back into the cap and a locking device engages, holding the line in place. When you release the button the locking device releases the line, allowing it to unwind from the spool and move freely around the cap.

When you turn the reel handle the pin pops out to pick up the line. As the cap revolves around the spool it winds the line back on it. The line rubs on the eye of the cover of the reel as it makes a sharp turn to go around the cap and then rubs on the revolving cap and pickup pin as it goes around it back to the spool. Both those points can be causes of problems.

If the line is not pulled tight coming out of the reel, the pin sometimes won't pick it up. It's best to hold the reel so your thumb and trigger finger can pinch the line in front of the cap and pull it tight as you start to reel.

Putting Line on a Spin-Casting Reel

Putting line on a reel correctly will solve many problems. If line is put on the wrong way it will twist and won't cast right. In spin-casting reels, twisted line will jam on the pin and inside the cover, making it difficult to clear without taking the cover off the reel. Light line works much better than heavy line on spin-casting reels. Ten-pound test is usually the heaviest line that should be used, and lighter is even better. The reel will have the suggested line size printed on it or in the instructions that come with it.

To put line on a spin-casting reel you must know which way the revolving cap turns. Open the cover and turn the handle to see the direction. While the cover is off the reel, run line from the tip of the rod up the guides, through the hole in the cover and then tie the line around the spool under the cap. Put the cover back on the reel and lay the new spool of line on the floor. If the cap in the reel is turning clockwise when observed from behind, lay the spool of line on the floor so the line unwinds from it clockwise, too.

Most new reels come with line on them. Take the cover off and notice the way the line is wound tight on the spool, how full the spool is, and which direction it runs. This will help when you have to put new line on the reel.

Hold the line tight between your thumb and trigger finger and reel the new line onto the spool. Holding the line tight makes it tight on the spool and less likely to cause problems. Fill the spool to one-eighth inch below the lip. Putting on less line will make it drag and interfere with casting; putting on too much will make it hang on the cap and not cast at all.

Spin-Casting Reel Quality and Drag

Reels can be made of many materials from steel to composites. They must be strong enough to hold up under constant use and light enough to balance the rod but not tire you out. Many cheap spin-casting reels are made of plastic with plastic gears. Avoid these. Metal gears are best for long-term usage and a metal cover will hold up better than plastic. The handle should be large enough to grasp comfortably and turn easily. Make sure it's not so small it bumps your hand as you turn it.

The drag system should allow line to be pulled off the spool smoothly and evenly, without any jerks. Pull line from the reel and adjust the drag until the line slips easily, then tie the line to a solid object and pull against it making the rod bend. The drag should slip and allow line to come off the reel when the rod is bent. You can attach a scale to the line and pull, adjusting the drag to slip at two-thirds to three-fourths the breaking point of the line.

Advantages and Disadvantages of Spin-Cast Reels

These are some advantages to using spin-casting reels:

- Spin-casting reels are cheap so they're not a big loss if children break them or throw them in the lake.
- It's easy to learn to use spin-casting reels.
- They can be either right- or left-handed, and some have handles that can be moved from one side to the other.
- A good-quality spin-casting reel will last a long time.
- Spin-casting reels can handle extremely light line and are a good choice for two- and four-pound test ultralight fishing.

These are some disadvantages to using spin-casting reels:

- Spin-casting reels are not good for heavy line or fighting strong fish.
- You're limited to light line, and the drag system isn't as good as it is on other kinds of reels.
- It's hard to keep the line tight on the spool.

- Twisted or loose line will jam the reel and you have to take the cover off to correct the problem.

Spinning Reels

Spinning reels are also called open-faced reels and work well in a wide range of fishing situations. They hang under the rod, and a bail (a U-shaped part that guides the line onto the spool) revolves around a fixed spool to take in the line. You can buy spinning reels designed for fresh and salt water, and some saltwater models hold large amounts of line, allowing them to be used for surf-casting and for fighting fish that make long runs.

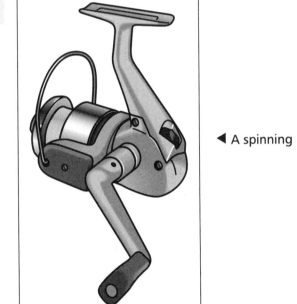

◀ A spinning reel.

How a Spinning Reel Works

The line is exposed on a spool sticking forward of the reel seat. A wire bail is mounted on a sleeve that revolves around the spool. This bail has a line guide spindle on it and it can be opened to allow the line to be cast. It locks open and stays there out of the way while the cast is made. When the handle is turned the bail flips back to the closed position, picking up the line and guiding it to the spindle. The line goes around the spindle and onto the spool.

FACT

Some spinning reels have interchangeable handles that will move from one side to the other. There is a hole or a threaded pin on both sides and the handle will fit on either one. The side not being used has a cap to protect the handle attachment.

The line comes up the rod guides and makes one turn under the bail spindle to go to the reel. As you turn the handle the spool goes in and out a short distance to make the line fill the spool evenly and not stack up. Drag on a spinning reel can be made (as a part of the spool) into the spool or in the reel itself. Center-drag reels have an adjustment for drag on the spool and the drag works between the spool and the reel housing (by creating friction between the spool and the reel and letting the spool turn and allow line to go out slowly as the fish pulls). Rear-drag reels have an adjustment on the back of the reel and the drag is internal (putting pressure on the stem that holds the spool on the reel and letting the spool turn slowly from this friction).

Putting Line on a Spinning Reel

Line should go on a spinning reel the same way it comes off the new spool. Lay the spool of new line on the floor and run the end of the line through the line guides on the rod, from the tip up to the reel. Leave the bail open and tie the line to the spool. If you forget to open the bail first, the line will not be under it and you can't retrieve it.

ESSENTIAL

If you forget to open the bail, unsnap the spool from the reel, open the bail, and then replace the spool. This is usually much easier than cutting the line from the spool and starting over.

From the rod handle end, look at the way the bail revolves on the spinning reel. If it turns clockwise, lay the spool of new line on the floor so it comes off in a clockwise direction. Hold the rod above the reel and turn the reel handle to close the bail. Start winding line onto the spool, letting the line run between your fingers, and keeping tension on the line so it spools tightly and evenly.

ALERT!

If the line starts to twist and form loops at the tip of the rod, the new spool of line on the floor is turned wrong. Flip it over and start winding line on again. It should not twist as you spool it up.

Fill the spool to one-eighth inch of the lip. If you put too little line on the spool it will bind on the edge as you cast, reducing the length of your cast. If you overfill the spool, the line will "jump" off the spool when you open the bail and cause problems.

Set the drag on a spinning reel so the line slips before it breaks. Start by pulling the line from the reel and tightening the drag until it slips easily but with a steady smooth resistance. Then adjust the drag while the line and rod are under a load as they would be when fighting a fish by tying your line to a solid object and pulling against it with the rod bent. The drag should slip at two-thirds to three-fourths the break test of the line.

Spinning Reel Quality and Drag

A metal or composite frame, and metal gears inside the reel, are much stronger than plastic and will not break under a strong load. A light metal bail is best, too. The spindle must be hardened so the line will not cut it. Better reels have a spindle that turns as the line passes over it so it will not damage the line.

The handle on a spinning reel makes a big loop and the bail also covers a lot of area when it's turning. For that reason make sure the handle doesn't hit the bail or your hand holding the rod while the bail is turning. The reel seat must be on a stem long enough for the bail to clear your hand when in use.

Advantages and Disadvantages of Spinning Reels

These are some advantages to using spinning reels:

- They are easy to learn to cast and simple to use.
- The spools can be big enough to hold a lot of line.
- The line makes only one sharp turn to go on the spool, reducing the binding areas.
- Line comes off the spool fairly straight to the first guide when casting, lowering drag on the line.
- If there's a problem you can see it and get to it easier.
- The spool of a spinning reel can also be much larger than on a spin-casting reel, so it retrieves line faster.
- Spinning reels can have the handle on either side, allowing fishermen to cast with their dominant hand.
- You can cast and hold the rod with one hand and turn the handle with the other without moving your casting hand.
- The drag systems are good enough to handle long runs of strong fish, like bonefish, on light line.

These are some disadvantages to using spinning reels:

- It's easy to twist line with a spinning reel, especially if you wind while the drag is slipping.
- Loops of line often form at the spool when you start winding the line in, and they will tangle on the next cast and cause problems.
- Some people feel they can't get good leverage for a hook set.
- Spinning outfits don't have the ability to horse fish out of cover fast (meaning, to pull the fish out of a tight spot quickly).

Bait-Casting Reels

Bait-casting reels are often called casting reels and they're well suited for a lot of different kinds of fishing tasks. They sit on top of the rod and the line comes off a revolving spool. Bait-casters are a little more difficult to learn to cast and are famous for getting backlash, or a bird's nest, in the line. Prices range from very cheap to extremely expensive but there are a lot of moderately priced bait-casting reels that will last a long time.

FIGURE 5-3

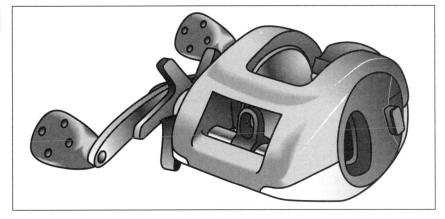

▲ A bait-casting reel.

How a Bait-Casting Reel Works

The spool on a bait-casting reel turns as you turn the handle, winding the line back on. A release button on the reel disengages the gears inside from the spool, allowing it to spin freely. After pushing the button to release the spool, you place your thumb on the spool to hold it in place while casting.

Keeping your thumb on the spool during the cast allows you to control the line flow precisely and make accurate casts. At the end of the cast you turn the handle to engage the gears between the handle and the spool, causing it to revolve and wind in the line. A line guide goes back and forth across the spool, laying the line evenly on the spool.

The drag system on a bait-casting reel is internal and engages the spool. It's usually made up of washers of different materials that rub together to cause friction to slow the turn of the spool. It can be very smooth and accurate, giving you a lot of control when you also use your thumb on the spool to add to the drag.

Putting Line on a Bait-Casting Reel

Line goes onto a bait-casting reel differently since the spool revolves. Run the new line from the tip of the rod through the rod guides and through the level wind guide on the reel. Tie the line to the spool and hold the rod between the first guide and the reel. Run the line between your fingers to keep it tight.

Stick a pencil through the hole in the filler spool and have someone hold it, or place it between your feet. Have the person holding the spool put some pressure on the spool, or let it rub on the floor as line comes off to keep it from spinning too fast. If the line is winding onto the reel spool over the top, make sure it's coming off the filler spool from the top, too. Wind the line on until the spool is filled to one-eighth of an inch from the top.

ESSENTIAL

Reels often hold more line than you want to use. You can save money and use less line to fill the spool by using backing under the good line. Pull off as much of the old line as you want to replace and tie the new line to it. Then fill the spool from that point with new line.

Bait-Casting Reel Quality and Drag

High-end bait-casting reels are made with frames of composite material to make them light, and the gears are hardened metal to make them last. The gears are especially important because they engage and disengage to cast, so they must mesh repeatedly without being damaged. Cheaper reels will strip gears and not last long.

Drag systems on bait-casting reels are layers of different materials that rub against each other to produce friction. They can be some of the smoothest in any kind of reel. Since you can use your thumb to add drag when a fish is fighting, you can set the drag initially to a lighter setting. That helps with fish that make long runs because less line on the spool means more drag. It is easier to add drag with your thumb than to adjust to reduce it while fighting a fish.

Advantages and Disadvantages of Bait-Casting Reels

These are some advantages to using bait-casting reels:

- Work better with heavier line
- More control while casting
- More control while fighting a fish
- Less line twist during normal use
- More power fighting strong fish

These are two disadvantages to using bait-casting reels:

- More difficult to learn to use
- More expensive than most other kinds of reels

Although you probably won't start out with a bait-casting reel, it's a good idea to get one and learn to use it. You should definitely have at least one bait-casting reel if you have more than one reel.

FACT

Bait-casting reels are harder to learn to use but give you the most control of any reels. You can use your thumb to control the line going out on a cast and to control the drag. It is worth the extra time it takes to learn to use a bait-casting reel for the added control it gives.

Combos

A combo is a rod and reel already put together and ready for use. It's a supplier's best guess at what best suits the customer. Many tackle stores offer combination rod and reel sets, some assembled by the manufacturer and some assembled by the store. You can also find them in fishing supply catalogs.

When you buy a combination outfit you get a matched set that's usually cheaper than the same rod and reel bought separately. But you have few choices and if either the rod or reel is not what you want, you'll be disappointed. Combos are usually in the middle range for fishing a wide variety of lures and situations so you often can't find them for specialized types of fishing.

FACT

A combination rod and reel set should be balanced. Check it by placing the outfit on your extended finger. It should balance just in front of the reel. If the outfit is heavy on either end, it will cause problems. Check outfits you put together yourself this way, too.

Fly-Fishing Reels

Fly-fishing reels are used to hold the line and are not part of the casting process. You strip line from the reel and it lies at your feet while casting, feeding out when you need it. This loose line is controlled by your free hand while your other hand holding the rod makes the cast. You don't touch the reel while casting with a fly-fishing outfit.

FIGURE 5-4

◀ A fly-fishing reel.

For most freshwater fishing, fly-fishing reels are not as important as they are in most other kinds of fishing, because retrieving line and fighting the fish are done with your hand. Line is stripped in with your free hand and that hand controls drag when setting the hook and fighting a fish. This is not true when fighting strong saltwater fish or freshwater fish that make long runs. With them, the drag on a fly-fishing reel becomes important just like on other reels. Special fly-fishing reels are made with good drag systems for fighting big-game saltwater fish and freshwater fish like steelhead. You fight them by controlling the line with your hand for the few seconds it takes them to pull all the slack out; then you start fighting them with the reel just as you would with other kinds of reels.

There are two kinds of fly reels, manual and spring loaded. With the manual reel, a handle is either attached directly to the line spool or moves it through a drag system. You reel line in by turning the handle. With the spring-loaded reel, you wind up the spring and the spring turns the spool when activated with a lever in front of the reel. This spring also acts as a drag system, but it's limited.

Costs of Reels

Reels can cost a few dollars to almost $1,000, and you probably don't want or need one at either end of that range. Cheap reels are worth what you pay for them and won't hold up. High-end reels are made for very specialized types of fishing for anglers who have a lot of money to spend, or who want to impress others more than they want to catch fish. Look for reels priced in the midrange for their type.

You can buy spinning reels for anywhere from $10 to $900, but very few are priced above $100. A good spinning reel that will last you for years can be bought for around $60, the midrange of the price of the majority of spinning reels.

Bait-casting reels are usually a little higher in price, ranging from the cheapest around $40 to several hundred dollars for top-of-the-line reels. You can get a bait-casting reel that will meet all your needs for less than $100.

A good ultralight spin-casting reel will cost you less than $15 and will do a good job. Some of the best spin-casting reels on the market cost less that $70, so they're much cheaper than other kinds of reels. Although many fishermen start with spin-casting reels, very few that fish a lot use them except for special types of fishing.

Fly-fishing reels can cost as little as $20 for freshwater reels to several hundred for saltwater reels designed to fight big-game fish. Many beginners find the spring-loaded reels easier to use but most experienced fly-fishermen prefer manual reels.

Good combo fly-fishing outfits can be bought for less than $100 and a very basic combo can cost as little as $30. Just remember that you get what you pay for, and this is very true with reels. Start with a good basic fly-fishing reel and you won't be disappointed.

For all reels, look for those made by well-known manufacturers that have been around for a long time and have established good reputations for quality products. They will usually stand behind their products if you have a problem, too. Also look at house brands from the big mail-order companies. They're usually good basic reels that will serve you well for a long time. And they're usually not very expensive for their quality.

Chapter 6

Make the Connection

The only thing between you and the fish is your line. If this connection fails, you won't land the fish. There are many kinds of lines and some are versatile while others have very specific applications. Choosing the right line will make your fishing easier and more productive.

What to Look for in Any Line

All fishing lines have certain characteristics that make them appropriate for certain types of fishing. Once you decide what kind of fishing you want to do and what rod and reel best suits your purpose, the next thing to consider is what's the best line to do the job. Here are the characteristics you need to consider:

- **Resistance to Abrasion:** How tough the line is, usually coded as extra-tough or extra-strong
- **Size:** The diameter of the line shown as hundredths of an inch or hundredths of a millimeter
- **Stiffness:** How flexible the line is, usually coded as limp or extra-limp
- **Strength:** The test of the line, shown as pounds of force needed to break the line
- **Stretch:** How much the line stretches when put under a load, usually coded as low stretch or no stretch
- **Visibility:** How easy it is to see the line, usually coded as high visibility, low visibility, or invisible

Monofilament Lines

Monofilament is the most common and widely used line. It's been around a long time, has proved itself over the years, and is the most inexpensive of the lines available. Many manufacturers offer it in a wide range of qualities. It can be colored or clear and is used for both saltwater and freshwater fishing.

ALERT!

Sun and salt water can damage monofilament lines. Avoid storing your reels and spare spools of line in the sun, and wash off the line on your reels after using it in salt water. Also avoid storing line where it gets very hot, like in the trunk of your car.

Monofilament is made by mixing a variety of chemicals together and heating them to form a gelatinlike substance. While still hot this gel is forced through tiny holes to form a string that is cooled quickly. The smaller the hole, the smaller and lighter the line will be.

The Qualities of Monofilament Lines

Monofilament can be manufactured to have different characteristics for different jobs. It can be limp for spinning reels, tough for fishing heavy cover, thin for fishing light lures, or thick for added strength. Color can be added so you can see it and watch for bites. Emphasizing one good quality often makes another undesirable quality more noticeable, though. If they're good lines for a wide variety of applications they'll have a general mix of all the characteristics, balancing out the good and bad. The higher-quality lines are usually formulated to meet specific applications and this information is often listed on the spool or box.

FACT

Monofilament line has "memory," which means it tends to keep the shape of the spool. Line that has been on the reel a long time will come off the spool in coils, making it hard to cast and even harder to detect bites. Keep fresh line on your reel.

Applications for Monofilament Lines

Use a thin, four- to eight-pound test line when fishing in clear water, on flats, and in shallow inshore waters. Spool it on spinning or spin-casting reels, and pair it with a light-action rod. Usually the thinner lines have more stretch so they don't break as easily when a fish makes a strong run near the boat. They also are more flexible which is better for spinning reels. Since they're lower test and have less abrasion resistance, they're not as good for bigger fish that like cover or for fishing cover like brush or shell beds.

Use higher test line that has more abrasion resistance for fishing in heavy cover or going after bigger fish. Brush piles, shell beds, and offshore rigs all call for abrasion resistant line. It will be stiffer so it will work better on a bait-casting reel and should be paired with a heavy-action rod. You will get less fight but you'll be much more likely to land a bigger fish.

For open-water game fish, especially hard-fighting saltwater fish, pick a line that has some stretch, to make break-offs less likely, and is thin relative to its test. Thinner lines cut through the water better and have less drag when fighting a fish with a lot of line out.

For most of your general fishing needs, especially saltwater fishing, choose a monofilament line. It's relatively inexpensive and you can change it often. Stick with brand names and don't buy so much line it will go bad before you can use it.

Avoid bulk spools unless you're spooling up a lot of reels or use a lot of line. You can't tell how long it's been sitting in the store and it won't be as good as fresh line if you keep it a long time. Buy spools of line that you'll use up in a few months.

Some professional bass fishermen change their line every day. There's no need for you to change yours that often, but change your mono-filament line as soon as it starts keeping coils, even if you used it for only a few casts. Old line holds memory even after it gets wet, which makes it more difficult for you to cast and feel bites. Strip off the first eighty feet of line and replace it with new line when this happens.

Braided Lines

Braids have been around for a long time, but they're more popular now that the fibers used to make them are extremely strong and abrasion resistant. Braided line is made by weaving strands of tough materials like Spectra or Micro-Dyneema into a tight strand of line. This weaving process is expensive and braids are some of the most expensive lines on the market. No other lines are as strong as the braids in relation to their diameter.

The Qualities of Braided Lines

Braids float and are easy to see since they are woven. They have no stretch and have a very small diameter for their strength. In fact, they're so strong and hard to break it can be a problem if you get hung up. They will cut your hands if you pull on them too hard.

QUESTION?

How can I break off a braid when hung?
Carry a short dowel or piece of broom handle a few inches long to wrap the line around before pulling. This will avoid cutting your hand with the line. In a boat, wrap the line around a cleat and use the motor to break it.

Extremely limp, they have no memory and hold up a long time. Even though they're very abrasion resistant, they're very abrasive themselves and require strong line guides and reel parts to handle them. They will cut into soft line guides, reel spindles, and level wind guides.

Special tools are needed to cut braids when changing lures and similar activities. A pair of very sharp scissors works best. Because they're so visible in the water, many people use a leader of monofilament or fluoro-carbon line to distance the bait from the braid. Braids must also be spooled tightly on the reel to keep the line from burying under itself. For this reason you have to make sure you reel line in under tension at all times.

Applications for Braided Lines

When you need a line that's super strong and doesn't stretch, and when visibility isn't important, braids shine. They're excellent for flipping since you need a heavy strong line, and most bites are reaction bites where the fish don't examine the bait long. Their limpness also allows the bait to fall straight down. "Flipping" is a method of making short "casts" by swinging a lure with about fifteen feet of line. You swing the lure to the target with the rod tip. It is a very similar method to fishing with a cane pole.

Braids are good for pulling big fish away from cover quickly. And they're are great for fishing around brush and rocks, which calls for a line that won't abrade easily and doesn't stretch, allowing the fish to get back into the cover. The only problem is if they hang up they won't break easily.

Braids are so tough you don't need a steel leader when fishing for toothy fish like muskie, barracuda, and pike. You can tie your bait directly to the line, eliminating the extra knot and hardware necessary for fishing with a steel leader.

More and more fishermen are using braids for big-game saltwater fish. Low stretch and abrasion resistance make it a good choice, but its tendency to bury into itself on the spool can be a problem. If you need to make a long cast in open water and set the hook in the mouth of a tough fish, use a braid. Tie on a three-foot monofilament or fluorocarbon leader and use a sharp hook. The low stretch will help you drive the hook home and the leader will keep the braided line away from the bait.

Choose a braid when you need its special qualities of abrasion resistance, no stretch, and limpness. It's very expensive, so don't try to fill your reel with it—use backing and tie just enough braid on top of it to make the longest cast you will need.

Braided Dacron Line

Dacron braid has been around for many years and is still used for big-game saltwater fish like marlin and tuna. It's not as slick as the new braids and won't bury itself into the spool of line like the new ones will. But it's not as strong as the new braids, although some fishermen prefer it for its ability not to bury into itself on the spool.

Fused Lines

Fused line has become very popular over the past few years. Fused line is made from the same fibers as braid line but the bundles of strands of the line are fused or glued together rather than woven. The individual fibers are extruded and fused together while still hot, and then they're coated with a gluelike material to hold them together. Using more or fewer strands of fiber determines the test of the lines.

FACT

With use, the coating will wear off fused lines, giving them a dull, rather than shiny, look. You may be able to see "fuzz" on the line as the fibers stick out. This doesn't weaken the line and it's still useful. Some say it's even better after it wears because it's more limp.

The Qualities of Fused Lines

Fused lines are very slick and thin for their strength. They have almost no stretch and don't break down when exposed to sunlight like some lines do. It's more abrasive resistant than monofilament lines but not as resistant to abrasion as braids. It's a little stiff when new but quickly becomes very limp with use.

For line watchers, fused lines are very good. They often come in bright colors that you can see and watch for bites. Although there are some colors that blend in with the water, fused lines are much more visible than some other kinds of line. Line-shy fish may avoid them and become very difficult to catch.

Like braids, fused lines have properties that can cause problems. They're very tough and thin and will cut your hand if you pull on them. And they'll slip on the reel spool because they're slick. Always use a backing of monofilament line under fused lines, or tape the line to the reel spool with black electricians tape after tying it on. Both methods will keep it from slipping on the spool.

The cost of fused lines has come down as they become more popular and are made by more companies. Fused lines cost a little more than monofilament lines but last much longer. They can be cost effective since you don't have to replace them as often.

ALERT!

Fused lines are so slick the knot can slip on them. Add extra wraps when tying an Improved Clinch knot or a Trilene knot. Palomar knots seem to work well with fused lines. Add a drop of super glue to the knot to make sure it holds without slipping. (See Chapter 8 for more about these knots.)

Applications for Fused Lines

Fused line is thin and flexible enough to work well on spinning reels that handle light baits better. The thin diameter and strength of fused line makes it good for fishing around vegetation because it will cut right through stems of lily pads and other plants and help you land the fish without balling them up in the grass or abrading the line.

And fused lines hold up well when rubbing against wood. This makes it very good for skipping baits under boat docks. Choose a fused line when you need a slick, strong line that doesn't have much stretch. Use it when fish are not line-shy since they can see it, and for fishing very light lures because it's so limp.

Fluorocarbon Lines

Fluorocarbon lines have been used in salt water for years but are becoming more popular in fresh water. These lines disappear underwater and become invisible to fish. They're very useful when fish are line-shy and you don't want to spook them.

The Qualities of Fluorocarbon Lines

Lines made of 100 percent fluorocarbon are the most invisible lines but they have other qualities that make them less useful. They're stiffer and less manageable on reels so they don't cast as well as other lines. And they are not as strong as other lines of the same diameter, but are still very tough and resist abrasion well. They're slick so they don't hold knots as well as some lines. They have a relatively large diameter and low stretch.

Applications for Fluorocarbon Lines

Use fluorocarbon lines in extremely clear water where you need a line that is completely invisible to the fish or whenever you go after line-shy fish. For flats fish like bonefish in salt water, invisible line can make the difference between catching fish and getting casting practice.

These lines also make good leaders for bait rigs and Carolina rigs (see Chapter 9 for more about rigs). The short length of the leader eliminates the problem with their stiffness. You spool another line that is easier to cast on your reel but still have the advantage of an invisible line between the bait and the main line.

Copolymer Lines

Copolymer lines are made by mixing two or more kinds of materials together, and, while they are fluid, extruding this blend through a small hole. They're actually monofilament lines because the end product is only one filament, but they're different from normal monofilaments since the materials are paired to produce blends for special qualities. Often a blend of polymers will give the best characteristics of each one while lowering its bad characteristics. Copolymer lines can be useful in a wide variety of applications or be made for very specific situations.

The Qualities of Copolymer Lines

Copolymers can have a wide variety of qualities depending on how the materials are blended. Many are blended to combine flexibility with strength and abrasion resistance. They can be thinner but stronger than regular monofilament but will usually be a little stiffer. They often have more memory than monofilament lines, but usually have less stretch. Visibility can be lowered in copolymers, too, giving them many qualities fishermen need while sacrificing only a little of the good qualities.

Applications for Copolymer Lines

Copolymer lines are appropriate for fishing anything from plugs to plastic worms and live bait in fresh water, to jigging spoons in salt water. If you have just a couple of reels, one should have a copolymer on it for all-purpose fishing. Heavier copolymers work best on bait-casting reels, and lower-test copolymers can be used on spinning reels.

Fly-Fishing Lines

Fly-fishing lines are a special case because you cast the line, not the bait. Fly lines are made of a variety of materials and must be strong enough to hold the fish and heavy enough to cast. They must also be soft and flexible so they spool easily and can be handled without problems. Their surface must be slick so it goes through the guide on the rod easily.

Since leaders are used to separate the fly line from the fly, a fly line can be very thick and made to perform a variety of jobs. Some fly lines float to help keep the bait near the surface, while others sink to take the bait down. Some have lead cores to take a fly to the bottom fast. They often come in bright colors to make it easier for the angler to see them. Some fly lines can be used in both fresh and salt water but usually fly lines are made for very specific tasks.

Lines Come in All Colors

Line colors can be confusing. From the bright colors of fused lines to the near invisibility of fluorocarbons, you can find just about any color you want. Some lines have a fluorescent material added so they have a soft glow in sunlight.

Use the least visible line you can when fishing live or prepared bait and lures that the fish see for a long time. When fishing a reaction bait like a jig, color matters less. Color can be important when you need to watch your line for a bite, so choose a color you can see. (E)

Chapter 7

Where to Buy Fishing Equipment

Sometimes it seems every gas station and convenience store has a shelf of fishing equipment. But when you need a specific lure or type of live bait you can search for days before finding it. There are many places to buy tackle that range from bait stands near fishing holes to the Internet. All have their good and bad points and are worth knowing about.

Mom-and-Pop Stores

Years ago every little town had a store that sold fishing equipment—and gas, groceries, hardware, and clothes. The owner was usually behind the counter and he fished when he could. That meant he knew what tackle was working and kept up with the newest innovations as well as where the fish were biting. He could advise you on what you needed and where to use it to catch fish. These kinds of stores still exist but are hard to find today.

FACT

As discount stores opened up many of the small tackle stores went out of business. The big chains could undersell them on any of the items they carried, so mom-and-pop type stores closed down. They can be hard to find now.

What You Will Find in Mom-and-Pop Stores

Walking into a mom-and-pop tackle store is often like walking into a time warp. Many of them are in old buildings away from the main part of town and a lot of them look like they haven't changed in a very long time. The cash register might really be a cash register, not a modern electronic machine, and you can bet items will be rung up by hand, not scanned in. And they smell like fishing, with the distinct odor of live bait, old wood, and musty undisturbed shelves.

ALERT!

It's easy to get distracted and talk for a long time about fishing in a store like this. Be careful that you don't lose track of time and forget what you came for.

The proprietor, who has probably owned the store for many years, may have as much character as the store and knows every item in it. Family members are often part of the management, helping out behind the counter. And don't be surprised to see several old men sitting or standing around talking about past fishing trips.

You will see counters covered with lures lined up in all the colors of the rainbow. A wall rack will usually hold bag after bag of plastic worms, arranged by manufacturer. There will probably be shelves of fishing clothes in the back, and rods will stick up from their racks on one side of the store. Near the back you'll hear the hum of the aerator in the minnow tank and crickets will chirp at you from their box.

A refrigerator will double as a earthworm cooler and a place for cold drinks. Behind the counter you'll see the expensive items including reels and knives. A whole section will be devoted to hooks, sinkers, and corks. Most of them will be loose in boxes rather than prepackaged, and you can scoop up the exact number you want. And there is likely to be a stack of helpful brochures from the state Department of Natural Resources.

The Pros of Mom-and-Pop Stores

When you visit them you'll most often be dealing with the owner, a person knowledgeable about fishing and what is good locally. The store will carry the items most often used in that area and the bait and tackle offered is what works. And you may well find some local fishermen hanging around who are willing to give you helpful information.

A variety of locally popular live bait is almost always a staple at this type of store. The owner can tell you how to keep it alive and fresh, the correct way to put it on the hook, and even how deep it should be fished. Different kinds of containers for bait will be available, from minnow buckets to cricket boxes, so you can carry them with you.

You might be able to find a treasure in one of these stores, too. Although you're unlikely to find a valuable lure (collectors have probably already checked it out), you may be able to find a selection of old plugs and other items no longer made. This kind of store is a good place to find your favorite discontinued reel, plug, or plastic worm, and stock up on it one last time.

Mom-and-pop store owners often can special order a hard-to-find item. They're usually willing to take the time to find and order something for you, so if you can't find what you want, ask if they can order it.

The owner of a small store will probably help you match up a rod and reel and even walk outside and make a few casts with a practice plug. The owner can show you how to balance a rod and reel and what pound test line to put on it. If you're real lucky the owner might even ask you to go fishing with him or her to try out your new equipment. This is much more likely to happen if you're a regular customer and you get to know the owner and the other people who work there.

Although parking is usually limited at these stores, it's close to the store and very convenient. You won't have to walk long distances with your purchase and these stores usually aren't crowded, making access much easier and less hectic that at bigger stores.

The Cons of Mom-and-Pop Stores

Small stores charge higher prices than the bigger stores. Since they usually order small numbers at one time, their cost is higher and they have to pass it on to you. Their markup probably isn't high enough to be able to bargain with you or put things on sale. Although these stores carry what's popular locally, it is unlikely they carry items you'll need on a trip out of the area. And they're less likely to carry really expensive items like high-quality reels, although they'd certainly order them for you. But that means you'll have to wait instead of walking out of the store with what you want.

FACT

You're likely to pay list price on most items at mom-and-pop stores, but you can get personal assistance and good local information that helps offset the higher prices. And if you special order an item you may even have to pay shipping on it, so make sure you know the total price before you order.

Discount Stores

The big discount stores usually carry a large selection of fishing equipment at low prices, and offer fishing licenses, too. These stores can be found on a main road near the edge of any good-sized town in the United States.

Be careful in all discount stores but especially in the ones that carry really cheap things. Some of the close-out stores have off-brand tackle that's not very good. Look for brand-name lures and equipment when buying at stores that have sharply discounted fishing equipment.

What You Will Find in Discount Stores

When you walk into a big discount store you can spot the fishing section by the forest of rods sticking up near the ceiling. Head to that area and you'll find dozens of rods of all kinds, many with reels attached in balanced combos. There are usually shelves and racks of every kind of fishing lure imaginable. Most everything is prepackaged and will be scanned into the computer checkout system by a clerk who probably doesn't know the difference between a hook and a sinker.

There are often several aisles of fishing equipment arranged in some kind of order. Plugs will be on one side of an aisle and plastic worms on the other. Line will be in another section where you'll find a wide choice of brands, kinds, and tests. There's usually even a section of freeze-dried and prepared baits for you to choose from. Everything will be clean and new because these stores turn over tackle fast, or get rid of it at the end of the season.

The Pros of Discount Stores

Prices at discount stores are usually cheaper than just about any other kind of store. They usually carry a good selection of fishing equipment, and you'll probably be able to find items that can be used for any kind of fishing, not just what's popular in that area. And these stores stay open long hours, so if you need something late at night before a fishing trip, you can probably get it.

You can take the whole family, and everyone can go to their favorite section to shop while you look at fishing tackle. Since these stores often offer everything from groceries to toys, there's something for everyone. That usually means, if others are along, you can spend more time looking at fishing stuff and they won't be begging you to leave.

The Cons of Discount Stores

Discount stores seldom carry live bait so don't expect to find any there. The people working at these stores usually don't know much about fishing and are there to restock shelves and keep things clean. They're not able to order specialized items and are limited in what they can stock. If you pick up a rod and reel to try out you may be asked to put them back and leave the merchandise alone. It's unlikely you'll be permitted to put a reel on a rod, fill the spool with line, and make a few casts with a practice plug.

Parking and shopping at a huge discount store can be hectic. Just finding a parking spot can drive you crazy, and once inside, the crowds aren't what fishermen usually enjoy. You'll have to walk a long way to get to the fishing stuff, going by way too many other tempting items in sections of the store you have to pass through.

ALERT!

Be sure to keep your cash register receipt and any tags from any item you buy. If you find you need to return it for any reason, having both items will help.

Mail-Order Catalogs

Looking through a catalog of fishing equipment, picking out the things you need, and then sending off an order can be an exciting way to shop for tackle. And the thrill of opening the package when it arrives is almost as good as Christmas. The items are usually priced low and you can find just about anything you want in a catalog.

What You Will Find in Mail-Order Catalogs

When you open a catalog you'll find just about any kind of fishing equipment available in many colors and sizes. Page after page of plugs, depth finders, trolling motors, and even boats are shown to their best advantage.

FACT

Tackle manufacturers buy pages in catalogs to display their products. Those willing to pay big bucks have several pages of items, but the smaller manufacturers can't afford this and their products may not be shown even if available. If there's an item you want to order but it's not shown, ask about it.

The Pros of Mail-Order Catalogs

Prices are good in mail-order catalogs. You can find just about anything you want and get it at some of the lowest prices around. It's fun going through a catalog and marking items you want and making a wish list. The marked catalog can be left for others to find when a birthday or Christmas is near.

Catalogs show good pictures of fishing tackle and you can usually choose from any color or style made by that particular manufacturer. Catalogs can contain merchandise from a huge number of companies and show more than just about any store could display. And they are convenient—you can look at them anytime you have a few minutes and do it in the comfort of your home.

In some cases, you also can save some money on sales tax when ordering by mail. If you order from another state, and the mail-order company doesn't have a store in your state, you don't have to pay sales tax on the items. This may mean a few pennies on a plug but on an expensive item like a trolling motor it can be significant.

The Cons of Mail-Order Catalogs

When ordering from a catalog it takes time to get what you want; you can't walk out of the store with it immediately. And you can't handle the items and test them; you can only look at them. There's no way to determine if an item is exactly what you want and no way to try it out beforehand.

Shipping and handling can get expensive on mail-order merchandise. This is especially true when you order a small number of items. When ordering a few plugs the shipping and handling can run the cost up higher than the marked prices at local stores.

Returning merchandise can be much more difficult when ordering by mail, too. Although some companies include a label to return the merchandise, you usually have to go to the post office and pay postage to send it back. And there's a delay between shipping the merchandise and getting credit for it, and if it gets lost in the mail you may be held responsible, unless you purchased insurance from the post office or paid for a return receipt.

Internet Stores

Internet stores are very similar to mail-order catalogs, with many of the same benefits and drawbacks. These types of businesses have really increased in number in recent years and there are a lot of them out there to choose from. Many are so new that they don't have a proven track record and it can be a problem getting what you order. But a lot of small manufacturers can be found on the Internet that supply their products directly to you.

What You Will Find at Internet Stores

Search the Internet for fishing tackle and you will get hundreds of sites, all claiming to offer merchandise at low prices. Many of the sites allow you to browse their products and give good descriptions as well as pictures of the items. Some specialize in one kind of product while others offer everything you could possibly need. You'll also find some sites set up by small manufacturers showing the tackle they make, and this is often the only way to find them.

The Pros of Internet Stores

It's easy to search the Net and find a lot of tackle for sale. The items listed can be changed quickly to respond to shortages and increased demand, something catalogs can't do. New tackle on the market can often be found at Internet sites before your local stores get it in stock. Very small suppliers can show you their merchandise with little expense and not have to pass on the cost of advertising to you.

Custom rod makers are a good example of the type companies that do well selling through the Internet. Although they may make only a few dozen rods a year, they can show their products and get information to you at a low cost to them. The Internet is about the only way to find out about such small companies.

Many of the bigger mail-order houses also have Internet sites. You can go to them and quickly find out what's in stock and order it faster than by mail. Dealing with the big companies that have been around a long time and have established themselves in other ways helps ensure good service.

The Cons of Internet Stores

Since Internet sites are so easy to set up, many are so small they don't have the ability to offer a wide variety of merchandise. And they may not stock anything, so it may take you a long time to get anything you order. If there's a problem it can be more difficult to solve since so many of these companies disappear overnight. Few of them have been around long enough to establish a good reputation.

You can't try items out; you must make your purchase by looking at a picture. This is not a problem if you know exactly what you want but it limits your ability to choose among several similar products. Returns can be difficult, too, and you'll have to have a credit card to make purchases.

Internet Auctions

Fishing tackle is a popular auction category on the Internet. At any time you can find hundreds of items ranging from rods and reels to tackle boxes full of lures. Prices start low and you can get bargains, but you can also get caught up in bidding fever and spend more than you want.

What You Will Find at Internet Auctions

People sell tackle on the Internet ranging from brand-new to well-used items. Just about anything related to fishing can be found there at times, and items change every day. To catch items you might want to buy, you have to keep a constant check to know what's being offered. Most auction sites allow you to search for things so you can narrow your selections. You can quickly pick out specific tackle or look at a lot of different things. Some single items are auctioned, but you'll often find tackle boxes and packs full of fishing gear.

The Pros of Internet Auctions

You can often find good bargains on Internet auctions sites. You can bid any amount you're willing to spend and buy what you want for less than it would cost you in a store. If you like auctions, the excitement of bidding on tackle can be enjoyable and exciting.

The Cons of Internet Auctions

You can't actually check out the merchandise you're bidding on and you must depend on the person offering it to be honest. The tackle may be used and not in as good condition as advertised. And the shipping might be very expensive and slow.

ALERT!

Before you bid on items on Internet auctions, be sure to check out the record of the seller. The better sites accept feedback from both buyers and sellers and you can get an idea of what to expect from them.

Be very careful about buying items on Internet auctions. Although you might get a good bargain, always remember the warning "buyer beware." Check out as much information as you can and start slowly. Ⓔ

Chapter 8

Tying One On

Your fishing line is the only thing between you and the fish, and your knot is what keeps the line attached to the hook. Many fish are lost because of knot failure. Learn to tie a good knot and you'll eliminate one possible weak link in your attachment to the fish.

Improved Clinch Knot

The Improved Clinch knot has been around for a long time and many fishermen use it. It's a strong knot that is adaptable to many different kinds of fishing. This knot can be tied with more or fewer loops depending on the type and test of line you're using. The Improved Clinch knot is a good basic knot to know and use.

When to Use the Improved Clinch Knot

Use the Improved Clinch knot to attach hooks, plugs, and spinnerbaits to all kinds of line. It works well with monofilament lines as well as some of the newer superlines. This knot is good in salt water and fresh water and will hold up to 95 percent of the line test if tied right. It can also be used to attach line to reels since it slides tight, and you can attach two lines to each other with it. It works best on thinner-diameter line and is hard to tie on very thick line.

FACT

Monofilament line will cut itself with the wrong kind of knot. A good knot in monofilament must have coils that cushion it from itself, like the Improved Clinch knot does. A simple Overhand knot in monofilament will reduce its strength by half.

Since the Improved Clinch knot pulls tight against the eye of the plug or hook, it will not allow the bait to move freely. Always use a snap or split ring on plugs and top-water baits, or use a loop knot, so they can swing as they are supposed to do. The Improved Clinch knot will dampen their movements if tied directly to the eye of the plug.

How to Tie the Improved Clinch Knot

To tie an Improved Clinch knot:

- Run the end of the line through the eye of the hook and pull about six inches through it.
- Wrap this tag end (the piece of six-inch line) around the standing line

three to seven times, going up the line away from the hook.

- Take the tag end and put it through the loop formed by the line at the eye of the hook.
- Bring the tag end back through the loop formed in the previous step.
- Wet the line with saliva at the knot.
- Pull on the standing line slowly and smoothly while holding the tag end, tightening the knot.
- When the knot is tight against the hook eye, pull on it very hard to make sure it's tight.
- Check to make sure the loops are stacked evenly and not on top of each other.

What is the standing line?
That's what we call the main line on the rod that extends from the reel to the hook.

QUESTION?

FIGURE 8-1

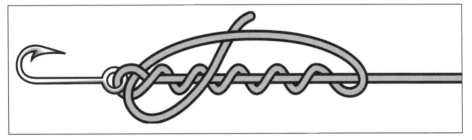

▲ Tying an Improved Clinch knot.

FIGURE 8-2

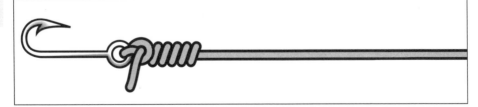

▲ A finished Improved Clinch knot.

A variation is to run the end of the line through the eye of the hook twice before starting to tie the knot. When tied like this the knot is sometimes called the Trilene knot. This is especially good with light line to give more contact with the hook eye and reduce the chance of it breaking there. When tying the Trilene knot you must pull the knot tight even more slowly since it's wrapping twice, and wetting it is even more important.

For very thin line or the slick lines like the fused lines, use seven loops around the main line. For thicker line reduce the number of loops to five. When tying line to reels you can even drop down to three loops since these knots don't have to be as strong.

When using fused lines add a little insurance to your knot by putting a drop of super glue on it after pulling it tight. Let the glue dry for a few seconds before casting. The glue will ensure that your knot will not slip.

Always wet an Improved Clinch knot with saliva when pulling it tight. This helps the knot tighten and not slip later. Also pull the knot very tight when tying it so it doesn't slip and break when you're fighting a fish.

Palomar Knot

The Palomar knot is one of the most popular with bass fishermen and is easy to tie. It holds well and will provide up to 95 percent of the breaking strength of the line when tied correctly. This knot is also the preferred knot to use when tying braided and fused line because it won't slip as easily as the Improved Clinch knot.

When to Use the Palomar Knot

Use the Palomar knot to attach hooks, plugs, spinnerbaits, and any other terminal tackle to your line. It's a little harder to use when fishing with big plugs because the plug must be moved through the loop while you're tying it, but it can be done. This knot also pulls down tight on the eye of the hook or plug so it's best to use a ring or snap-on free-swinging baits.

The Palomar knot is useful in saltwater and freshwater applications and, because it's a small knot, it's a good knot for tying on very small hooks and baits. You can tie on hooks for live-bait fishing as well as any kind of small terminal tackle with this knot. It's not recommended for tying two lines together because it would be almost impossible to tie correctly.

How to Tie the Palomar Knot

To tie a Palomar knot:

* Double about six inches of line at the end and stick the end of the loop through the eye of the hook or lure.
* Tie an Overhand knot in the doubled portion of the line and leave the bait hanging from the bottom of the loop that's formed when you tie it.
* Hold the Overhand knot between your finger and thumb and pass the hook through the loop at the end of the line.
* Keep your finger on the Overhand knot or between the hook and line, and start pulling the knot tight.
* Pull it tight by pulling on both the tag end and the standing line at the same time.

FACT

An Overhand knot is a knot made by making a loop in the line, inserting the tag end back through the loop, and pulling tight.

FIGURE 8-3

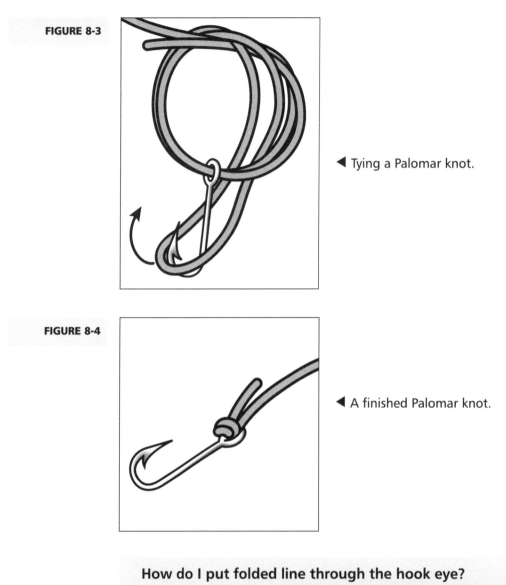

◀ Tying a Palomar knot.

FIGURE 8-4

◀ A finished Palomar knot.

How do I put folded line through the hook eye?
If the line will not go through the eye of the hook easily after forming a loop, stick the end of the line through the eye of the hook then stick it back through while holding the loop to make enough room.

QUESTION?

Uni Knot

The Uni knot is easy to tie, and you can do it almost with your eyes closed. It holds well in all kinds of lines and will hold at about 95 percent of the break test of the line you are tying it in.

When to Use the Uni Knot

Use the Uni Knot for attaching terminal tackle that doesn't swing freely to the end of the line. Although this knot can be tied to leave a loop at the end, the knot will slide tight when you hook a fish and this can weaken it. It's best to pull it tight while tying it and use a snap or split ring if the plug needs to swing freely. The Uni Knot works well in both saltwater and freshwater applications.

ESSENTIAL

On all knots, trim the tag end of the line about one-eighth inch from the knot. Don't try to cut it too short but don't leave it long enough to cause problems. You don't want to leave it so long that it catches trash in the V where it enters the knot.

How to Tie the Uni Knot

To tie the Uni knot:

* Hold the hook or plug in one hand and pass the end of the line through the eye of it.
* Run the tag end along the main line for about two inches then loop the tag end back to the eye of the hook.
* Start wrapping the tag end around the double line inside the loop formed when you bring it back to the hook eye.
* Wrap it six times; then pull the tag end tight.
* Wet the knot and pull it down tight against the eye of the hook and firmly pull on it to make sure it's snug.

FIGURE 8-5

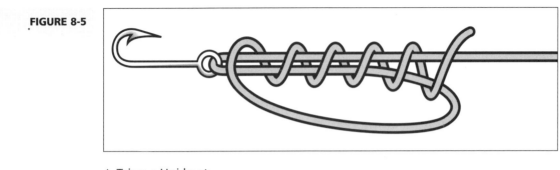

▲ Tying a Uni knot.

FIGURE 8-6

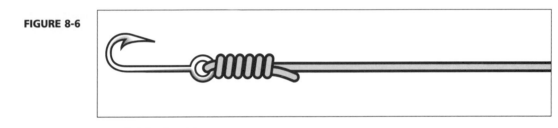

▲ A finished Uni knot.

FACT

All three of these knots—Improved Clinch, Palomar, and Uni—pull up tight on the eye of the hook or plug. They're all very similar and do the same job. Learn to tie any one of them and use it all the time; by using one of them all the time you'll learn to tie it better.

Rapala Knot

Also called a Brubaker Loop knot, this knot is a good one to tie to a plug that needs to move freely on the line. It leaves a loop at the end of the line so the eye of the plug is not held tightly and the knot doesn't dampen the lure movement. It's easy to tie and is a combination of the Overhand knot and the Improved Clinch knot. The loop can be left any size that you need it to be.

When to Use the Rapala Knot

Use the Rapala knot when tying on plugs like the floating Rapala that needs to move freely at the end of the line. This knot eliminates the need for a snap or split ring, so it's good to use when the lure is light and the weight of the snap or split ring might interfere with the action of the plug. Using a loop knot like the Rapala, rather than a snap or ring, also removes one place that a piece of equipment might fail while fighting a fish.

ALERT!

Tying an Overhand knot in your line usually will weaken it by as much as 50 percent, but the Rapala knot uses the loops of line running through the Overhand knot to cushion it. Otherwise, never tie an Overhand knot in your line, and always cut back to any that form while casting.

How to Tie the Rapala Knot

To tie a Rapala knot:

- Start by tying a loose Overhand knot about six inches up from the end of the line.
- After putting the tag end of the line through the eye of the lure or hook, put it through the loop formed by the Overhand knot.
- Twist the tag end of the line three to five times around the standing line above the Overhand knot, making a clinch knot; then bring the tag end back through the Overhand knot again.
- Return the tag end through the loop formed by the last step. At this point the tag end should be running the same direction as the standing line.
- Start pulling the tag end and standing line at the same time to tighten the Overhand knot and the clinch knot together.
- When the Overhand knot is tight, pull on the tag end to tighten the clinch knot.
- Make sure the loops are even and don't cross each other.

FIGURE 8-7

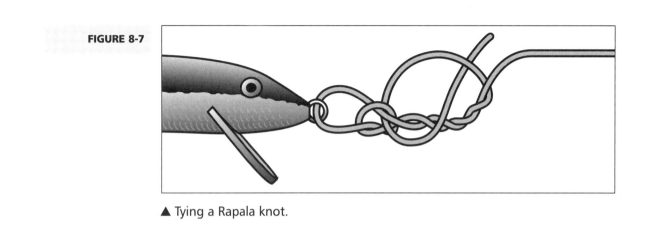

▲ Tying a Rapala knot.

FIGURE 8-8

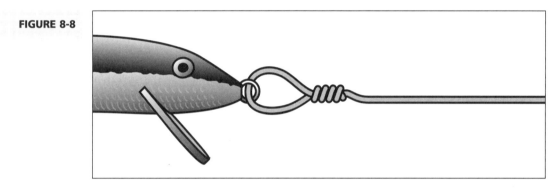

▲ A finished Rapala knot.

When tying a Rapala knot, you can make the loop any size you want by increasing or decreasing the distance between the eye of the plug and the Overhand knot. The loop will be the same length as the distance from the hook eye to the Overhand knot.

Surgeon's End Loop Knot

This knot is used to form a standing loop at the end of your line. It's very simple to tie and will hold the strength of the line well. The knot will not slip tight when you pull on it and the loop stays open even under a load. The Surgeon's End Loop knot has been around a long time, has been tested by many fishermen, and has proved itself often.

When to Use the Surgeon's End Loop Knot

Use the Surgeon's End Loop knot when you need a loop at the end of your line to attach hooks, leaders, or other lines. You can quickly attach a Snelled hook (see Chapter 9) or a lighter leader. You can use it to tie on a plug that needs to swing freely, but the Rapala knot is better for that purpose. This knot is best for tying an open loop with nothing on it when you tie the knot. You attach the tackle after tying the knot for the best results.

How to Tie the Surgeon's End Loop Knot

To tie the Surgeon's End Loop knot:

- Double the end of the line, making the doubled section a little longer than you want the loop to be.
- Start by tying an Overhand knot where you want the base of the loop to be, but don't tighten it down.
- Bring the end of the loop through the Overhand knot.
- Keep our finger in the loop and slowly tighten down the doubled Overhand knot.
- When it gets almost tight, wet it; then pull the loop while holding the standing line.
- Make sure the coils of the knot are even and not on top of each other.

FIGURE 8-9

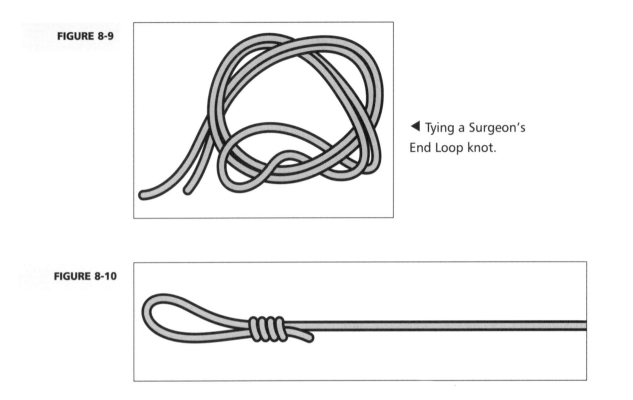

◀ Tying a Surgeon's End Loop knot.

FIGURE 8-10

▲ A finished Surgeon's End Loop knot.

Dropper Loop Knot

Sometimes you need to attach another line above the end of your main line. This can be done with a Dropper Loop knot and it will not weaken the line much. It will also not slip and let the line slide to the end of the standing line. It's used in fly-fishing, saltwater fishing, and freshwater fishing.

When to Use the Dropper Loop Knot

Use the Dropper Loop knot to attach a dropper line for a fly off the side of the leader, to attach a line above the sinker to move the bait away from the line on casting and spinning outfits, and to add a leader for a hook above the end of the line to keep the bait and hook off the bottom. The second two methods are useful when fishing rocky bottoms in both fresh and salt water. You can slide a slip sinker (a sinker with a hole through the middle) on the end of the line and peg it in place. Tie your hook to a line off the dropper knot and you can pull the lead off if it gets hung and not lose your hook and bait.

When fly-fishing you can tie a short dropper line off your leader well above the fly you're fishing and attach a dry fly that will dabble the surface like a mayfly or other insect laying eggs. This often works on reluctant trout to get them to hit because this isn't something they see often. And the dropper keeps the fly just at the surface or above it, keeping the trout from getting a good look at it.

For saltwater fishing a spreader rig (see Chapter 9) can be made by tying two of these knots above the sinker tied to the end of the line. Use heavy leader material and the droppers will stand out from the main line spreading out above the bottom. This is a good flounder rig.

How to Tie the Dropper Loop Knot

To tie the Dropper Loop knot:

- Make a loop in the line where you want the Dropper Loop to be.
- Pull the line from one side of the loop through the loop, keeping your finger in the original loop.
- Make five or more turns around the standing line with the loop you just formed.
- Push the end of the loop you're holding open with your finger through the new opening.
- Hold the line pushed through with your teeth and wet the knot with saliva.
- Pull both ends of the line away from the loop while continuing to hold it with your teeth.
- Release the loop and pull the ends of the line hard to tighten the coils evenly.

FIGURE 8-11

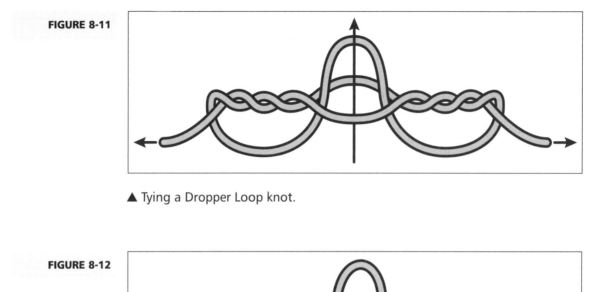

▲ Tying a Dropper Loop knot.

FIGURE 8-12

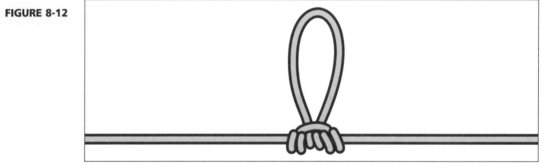

▲ A finished Dropper Loop knot.

Nail Knot

The Nail knot is used to tie fly-fishing line to a leader. It's been used for a long time and is a proven way to attach the two types of line. It takes some practice to learn and a hollow tube like a small straw is easier to use than a nail when tying this knot. Although it has been replaced by metal eyelets in many cases, this knot is still the best way to attach the line to the leader.

When to Use the Nail Knot

Any time you need to tie a leader to a fly-fishing line use the Nail knot. It makes a smooth connection that will not bind on the guides as it goes through them. This knot will also hold under pressure when fighting a fish.

How to Tie the Nail Knot

To tie a Nail knot:

- Use a nail (that's how the knot gets its name) or a small straw used to stir coffee.
- Lay the nail (or straw) beside the end of the fly line and put the end of the leader beside both of them. Leave at least twelve inches of leader line above the nail to use it to tie the knot.
- Hold the nail, leader, and fly line together with one hand and wrap the end of the leader around them six to eight times.
- Make the wraps close together and keep them even, working toward the end of the fly line and toward the leader.
- Push the end of the line you're wrapping back through the straw or beside the nail and then pull on it to tighten up the loops of line.
- Slide the nail out of the loops and then pull both ends of the leader line at the same time to snug it up.
- Pull hard on both ends of the line to tighten it up on the fly line; then trim off the end of the tag so it doesn't stick out.
- Pull on the leader while holding the fly line to make sure the line is strong and doesn't slip.

FIGURE 8-13

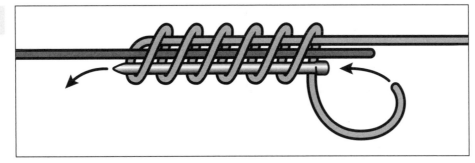

▲ Tying a Nail knot.

FIGURE 8-14

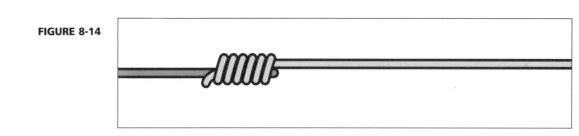

▲ A finished Nail knot.

ALERT!

This knot will not hold for any purpose other than attaching leader to fly line. The fly line is soft enough to hold it but others will not. Use a Blood knot or two Uni knots when tying other types of line together.

Blood Knot

A Blood knot is a good knot to use when tying two lines together that are about the same size. It's easy to tie but leaves a fairly big knot where the lines join. Fly-fishermen and saltwater fishermen use them to tie leaders together. This knot is time tested and is a very strong way to tie lines together.

When to Use the Blood Knot

Use a Blood knot any time you need to tie two lines of similar size together. They're also good for tying long fly-fishing leaders to different test lines, and making them fall straight. They are small enough to go through guides without much friction. Blood knots are also good to tie leaders in saltwater fishing when attaching lighter leaders to the main line.

How to Tie the Blood Knot

To Tie a Blood knot:

- Start a Blood knot by overlapping the ends of the two lines you are joining together.

- Twist one around the other at least five turns and then bring the end back between the two in the loop formed by the twist.
- Do the same with the end of the other line, going in the opposite direction; be sure to make the same number of turns with the second line as you made with the first line.
- Slowly pull the two lines in opposite directions and tighten the knot; watch to make sure the wraps slide together without lapping over each other.
- Pull it tight and clip the tag ends close to the knot.

FIGURE 8-15

▲ Tying a Blood knot.

FIGURE 8-16

▲ A finished Blood knot.

FACT

There are many more knots you can learn to tie, and many of them have special purposes. Sometimes it's fun just learning to tie a new knot and seeing how it works for you. Experiment with several and pick what does the best job for your fishing.

Chapter 9
Terminal Tackle

Although anything tied on the end of your line can be considered terminal tackle, this term usually applies to hooks, sinkers, floats, swivels, and other related items used for fishing live or prepared bait. This category includes a huge amount of tackle ranging from a simple hook tied to the end of the line to complex bait spreader rigs.

Hooks

You can find a hook in a size and style to catch anything from a minnow to a marlin. Hooks even come in a lot of different colors. Although the range of styles of hooks is huge, and there are myriad sizes of hooks in each style, a few basic sizes and styles will serve most of your fresh- and saltwater fishing needs.

The most important feature of a hook is how sharp it is. Some are extremely sharp when you purchase them but others need to be sharpened. A dull hook will not work well and will cause missed strikes and lost fish. No matter which type or size hook you use, make sure it's sharp.

Hook Size

Hook size is based on the gap between the shank of the hook and its shaft as well as the length of the shaft. It's expressed as a number and the larger the number, the smaller the hook—up to a point. A #22 hook is tiny and used for tying flies, a #6 hook with a quarter-inch gap is about right for bream. The size rule is consistent until you reach a #1 hook. The next bigger hook is a 1/0 and it goes up from there. A 2/0 is a good size for plastic worms for bass and a 10/0 is big enough for shark.

The length of the shaft of the hook is fairly standard, too. A #6 hook usually has a shaft about five-eighths to seven-eighths of an inch long. If the number of the hook is followed by another number and an x, that means the shaft is longer or shorter than normal. For example, "#6 2x Long" means this #6 hook has a shaft the length of a hook two sizes bigger. A #6 2x Short has a shaft the length of a hook two sizes smaller.

You choose a hook size based on the size of the mouth of the fish you want to catch. Although a five-pound carp and a five-pound bass are basically the same size, you use a much smaller hook for the carp because it has a much smaller mouth than the bass. You must also consider the size of the bait you're putting on the hook. Live minnows require a bigger hook than earthworms even when fishing for the same kind of fish because the gap in the hook needs to be large enough to allow the minnow to move.

Hook Style

Hooks are made in different shapes for different kinds of fishing. Some have a very wide gap between point and shaft to make it easier to use a thick plastic worm and still have a bit of a gap for the bait to fill when you set the hook on a fish. Some have barbs, special bends, and even small coils of wire to keep plastic worms or prepared bait on them. And they can be made of very heavy or very light wire, specialized for different kinds of fish.

A few styles of hooks include:

- **Aberdeen hook:** A round-bend light wire hook with a slightly turned-in point, used in many freshwater applications from live-bait fishing for bream to bass.
- **Bait Holder hook:** A hook with barbs on the shaft or a small spring attached to it, to help hold prepared bait on the hook.
- **Egg hook:** A short-shanked hook with a wide gap used for fishing with salmon eggs, dough balls, corn, and other prepared bait.
- **Offset Shank hook:** A hook with a shaft that bends in an L shape, mainly used to hold plastic worms on the hook.
- **O'Shaugnessy hook:** A strong round-bend hook that is used in a lot of saltwater applications like fishing live bait.
- **Sproat hook:** A widely used hook with a stronger parabolic bend rather than a round bend.
- **Weedless hook:** A hook with a wire or plastic weed guard running from the eye of the hook to the point to keep it from hanging up in weeds or debris.

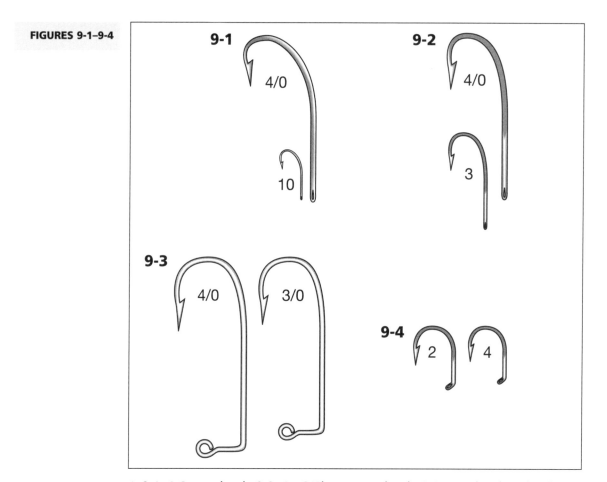

▲ 9-1: A Sproat hook. 9-2: An O'Shaugnessy hook. 9-3: An Aberdeen hook (shafts are bent for making lead head jigs). 9-4: An Egg hook.

Hooks are also made as double- and triple-gang hooks, meaning two or three hooks on one shaft. These hooks and have special uses and are very common. Take notice, the sizes on treble and double hooks can be different from single hooks. For example, a #4 treble hook won't always have the same gap as a #4 single hook.

FIGURE 9-5

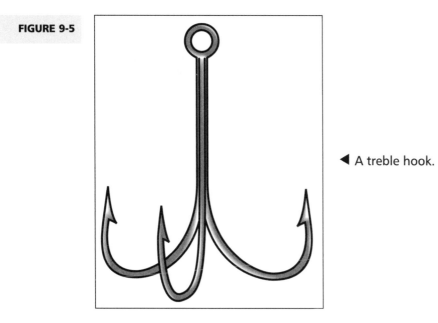

◀ A treble hook.

FACT

Most hooks have a barb below the point to keep it from coming back out of the fish's mouth after it goes in. Some hooks are made without this barb and some waters have rules requiring the use of barbless hooks. You can make a hook barbless by mashing the barb flat with a pair of pliers.

Hook Material

Most hooks are made of some kind of steel ranging from iron to stainless steel. Saltwater hooks generally are made of material that resists rust, while freshwater hooks don't need that protection because they don't rust as fast. Certain alloys help the hook stay sharp and others make it very tough so it will not bend when fighting a big fish.

ALERT!

Stainless steel hooks don't rust in your tackle box and they don't rust in a fish's mouth. When a fish is hooked deep in its throat many fishermen cut the line and leave the hook if they are releasing the fish, but that's a mistake with stainless steal hooks. A stainless steel hook may not deteriorate fast enough for the fish to live.

Snelled Hooks

A Snelled hook is any kind of hook with a leader tied to it in a special way. The line is not tied to the eye of the hook but to the shaft. Some Snelled hooks don't even have an eye; they have a spade-type foot at the end of the shank. The line is wrapped around the shaft of the hook and tied so it pulls in a straight line.

Snelled hooks have some advantages over regular hooks. The knot attaching the hook to the line is very strong and makes contact with the hook in more than one place, reducing the chance that it will break. And the way it's attached puts a more direct pull on the hook, giving you a better hook set and more control during the fight. The other end of the leader is usually tied in a loop so it can be quickly attached to your line with a loop knot or snap.

FIGURE 9-6

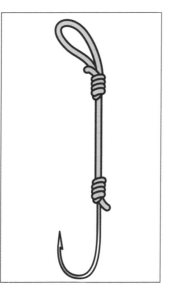

◀ A Snelled hook.

Sinkers

Sinkers are also called *lead* or *weights* and are used to get your hook down into the water. Several styles are made for various fishing methods and you can buy sinkers weighed in tenths of an ounce to pounds. They attach to your line in several different ways and they have many different shapes.

Sinker Size

Most sinkers come in sizes based on weight but Split Shot, one of the most popular kinds of sinker, is sized differently. Bullet Weight sinkers for bass fishing generally range from one-sixteenth of an ounce to one ounce, and Egg sinkers for fishing rivers may start at one-quarter ounce and go up to several ounces in weight. Saltwater sinkers used for halibut fishing in strong currents may weigh a pound each.

Split Shot and other small sinkers come in sizes ranging BB to 10 or higher, with the bigger numbers representing heavier sinkers. By keeping a combination of sizes and adding them in different sizes, you can fine-tune the weight on your line in very small increments. Split Shot can also be opened and removed so you can use it again.

FACT

Use the smallest sinker you can use and still get your bait where you want it. Use a heavy sinker for strong current, getting bait deep or making long casts. Never use more weight than you have to use since sinkers make the bait look unnatural and discourage bites at times.

Sinker Style

You can choose a sinker to crimp on your line, or to allow the line to move through it, or even one that will not hang up on the bottom as badly due to its shape keeping it from going into cracks in rocks. Shapes and styles are made for a lot of different purposes, some very specialized. Some of the most common include the following.

- **Bell sinker:** A bell-shaped sinker that has a way of attaching the line to the top of the bell, used for fishing below the hook and dragging on the bottom.
- **Bullet Weight sinker:** A bullet-shaped sinker with a hole through the middle, used for worm fishing for bass.
- **Egg sinker:** An egg-shaped sinker with a hole through it used for fishing in current and deep water.
- **Pyramid sinker:** A pyramid-shaped sinker used to dig in to soft bottoms of sand or mud to help hold a bait in place in current.
- **Split Shot sinker:** A round soft lead weight with a gap in it to put over your fishing line and pinch tight to hold it in place.

FIGURES 9-7–9-9

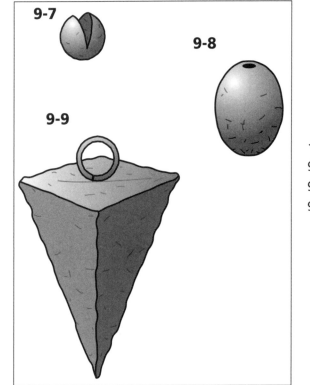

9-7

9-8

9-9

9-7: A Split Shot sinker.
9-8: An Egg sinker.
9-9: A Pyramid sinker.

Sinker Material

Lead has always been the most popular material for sinkers because it's soft and dense. New environmental concerns have forced the adoption of new materials like brass and cadmium, but these materials are much more expensive and don't work as well as lead because they are not as dense. Many of them are also hard and can't be used for Split Shot because they will cut the line if you force them closed on it. Stick with lead sinkers if they're allowed where you fish.

Floats

Attaching a float to the line to indicate a bite on the hook has long been a way to know when a fish is nibbling your bait. Floats not only show you when something is biting, they also can be used to suspend the hook at a certain depth where you think the fish are feeding, and to keep the bait out of trash on the bottom. When you're fishing water with a current, a float can carry your bait down the stream, offering it to many fish.

Kinds of Floats

For many years floats were made mostly of cork and many people still call them corks, no matter what they're made of. There are different shapes of floats for different kinds of fishing, too. Traditional cork floats are usually shaped like a bottle cork and have a split in the side to run your line through. Plastic floats come in all shapes and sizes, but round red-and-white ones have been the most common for a long time. They have a wire hook running through them with a spring to let them hold your line tight.

Styrofoam floats are very common now and they can be found in any shape you want. Round or egg-shaped floats are very common and they either have a spring-loaded clip or a hole through the middle for your line. Corks with a hole through them work well as slip floats or you can stick a small rod in them to hold your line in place. They're usually very colorful so they can be seen easily on the water.

Another name for floats is *bobbers* because that's the motion they have sitting on the surface of the water. It's very relaxing watching a bobber gently moving up and down with the ripples on the water, but it gets real exciting when the bobbing lets you know a fish is interested in your bait. Most kids find watching a bobber a good way to fish, so it is a good way to get them started.

Quill floats are long and thin and your fishing line attaches to one end. They will quiver and stand up with the slightest bite so they're used for match fishing and at other times when you need to detect the slightest nibble on your bait. The original ones were made from porcupine quills.

Other Uses for Floats

A float also adds weight to help in casting light bait. Some are even called casting bubbles and have a clip on each end to attach your main line and leader. A fly or very light bait can be added to the end of the leader and cast with spinning or even bait-casting equipment.

Some floats have concave faces at one end with a place to attach your main line and a tapered end at the other to attach the leader. When you pull the main line the float pops and gurgles in the water, attracting fish. The noise resembles fish chasing baitfish on the surface. These floats often have a lead weight in them to make them stand up and also to help in casting them long distances.

As with sinkers, use the smallest float that gets the job done. Don't try to suspend a cricket under a float the size of a softball because it will make too much noise hitting the water and its size may spook the fish. You'll need one that size to float a spreader rig across flats in bays when fishing for flounder, though. Match the size of your float to the job you want it to do.

Swivels

Swivels are used to keep your line from twisting. As you fish, the bait often causes your line to twist, and a swivel will prevent that from happening. Some baits don't twist as much as others, so you might be able to get by without a swivel for certain ones.

Look for quality swivels that spin easily. A barrel swivel can be made very simply and they are cheap, but higher-quality ones have a ball bearing in them and turn with very little pressure. They're usually stronger than the barrel swivel, too. Use them when fishing for hard-fighting fish, when trolling, or for any type of fishing when the bait spins a lot.

ALERT!

Use a black or dark swivel when fishing for species of fish that like to attack shiny objects. A bright silver swivel a foot up the line from the bait may attract the strike of a barracuda and not only will you not hook them, they will cut your line. You must use a swivel with some baits to keep your line from twisting.

A swivel can also be used to stop the lead and keep it away from the bait. This is the typical setup on a Carolina rig used for bass fishing. You thread a Bullet Weight on your main line and tie a swivel to it, then attach a leader from a few inches to several feet long. This keeps the bait away from the lead and can be used for live bait as well as plastic worms.

Regular swivels have a loop at each end to attach line to, but you can also buy three-way swivels that have three loops for the line. These swivels work well for bait walker rigs and any other time you need to tie more than one leader to a swivel. They're often not as strong as a regular swivel so make sure you get a quality three-way swivel if fishing for big fish.

Fish Finder Rigs

A fish finder rig is a good rig for catching fish that feed on or near the bottom in salt water and fresh water. This rig combines a swivel, lead, and hook to efficiently get your bait to the bottom and keep it in position without interfering with its action. For that reason, it works well with live bait as well as cut and prepared bait, and will work in still and flowing waters.

Start by tying a heavy swivel to the end of your main line. To the other eye of the swivel tie on a lighter leader twelve to thirty-six inches long, depending on how high you want your bait off the bottom (a lighter leader is a piece of line that is lower-pound test than the main line). Attach a Bell sinker to the end of this leader. Then tie another leader to the same eye if you're using a single swivel, or to the third eye if your using a three-way swivel. Attach your hook to this leader and bait it up.

> **What's a rig?**
> As the word is used here, it's a general term for specially prepared terminal tackle, but it can also refer to an outfitted boat.

QUESTION?

The hook leader can be any length you need it to be to allow the bait to work freely. If you want it near the bottom, make is as long or longer than the sinker leader. If you want to keep it up off the bottom tie it shorter than the sinker leader. As the sinker sits on the bottom or drags along, the bait will follow behind it slightly above it, depending on how long you made the hook leader.

This rig is great for drift-fishing or still-fishing. And if you have problems with the sinker hanging up, the lighter leader should break and allow you to reel in your hook and bait or any fish that hit. You can also use an Egg sinker on the end and either peg it with a toothpick or crimp on a Split Shot below it, rather than tying it to the leader. That way it will slide off the line when hung rather than break the leader. You can quickly slip another sinker on the end and be fishing again.

If your lead slips off too easily when holding it on with a toothpick, tie an Overhand knot in the line below the sinker before sticking the toothpick into the hole in the sinker the line runs through. This will make is slightly harder to pull off but not as hard as if a Split Shot is crimped on the line.

You can also add a float to a fish finder rig to help make it work better. When drifting over a flat bottom the float can keep the lead just bumping the bottom. If casting, use a slip bobber (a bobber with a hole through the center that allows the line to move freely) and you can detect bites. It will also help you reel in your rig because it pulls the hook and lead up to the surface and away from trash on the bottom that would hang it up.

Clips and Snaps

Swivels sometimes are paired with clips, (a snap that opens and closes) with one end of the clip attached to the swivel and the other end made into a clip so it can be opened and closed. This allows you to attach leaders, Snelled hooks, or lures easily without retying knots. You can also buy clips without swivels for attaching things to your line when you do not need a swivel.

Quality Clips

The better clips have a cross-locking system to make sure they don't come open when fighting a fish. The ends of the snap fold back and cross over the main part of the snap when closed, locking them into place. These kinds of clips can withstand a lot of pressure without opening.

Light wire clips are the best if they're made of strong material. The smaller, thinner ones don't add a lot of hardware to your line near the hook and won't spook the fish. Snaps should not be used with a hook when fishing for very shy species. In that case tie directly to the hook; the time spent retying knots will be well worth the added bites you'll get.

FACT

Snaps are too easy to open if bent or after a lot of use. Always replace bent or worn snaps to make sure they don't fail you when fighting a trophy fish. The cost of a new snap is not worth the chance of losing the biggest fish you've ever hooked.

Use a clip that's at least as strong at the line it's tied to. Stronger clips are usually bigger and there's no need to tie a big, strong clip to light line, but you need a strong clip on heavy line. If the line is too much stronger than the clip you'll pull it open when fighting a fish. It's best to avoid using a clip but if you need one, make sure it is tough enough so it's not the weakest point in the connection to the fish.

Bait Walkers

Bait walkers are specialized pieces of equipment that combine a sinker with a wire frame. The wire frame is usually V-shaped with a loop at the end of one arm of the V to attach a leader, and a loop at the point of the V to attach to your main line. The end of the other arm of the V will have a lead weight on it of varying weights, usually shaped like a banana. They work in a similar way to fish finder rigs.

When the bait walker is rigged up and dropped to the bottom, the lead weight "walks" along the bottom leaving the bait trailing above and behind it. The shape of the weight helps avoid hang-ups that more traditional sinkers would encounter. Bait walkers are very good for drift-fishing a bait along a flat for walleye or other similar species that hold near the bottom.

Bait Spreader Rigs

Another commonly used rig is the bait spreader rig. It allows you to fish two or more baits at the same time on the same line. They're much more common in salt water and usually are used for bottom-fishing, but some kinds are made for trolling several baits at once.

The spreader rig can look like a wire coat hanger without the bottom piece, or like a vertical wire with two arms sticking off it at different levels. In either case, a leader is tied to the end of each arm and a hook tied to each leader. At the bottom of the vertical wire or in the center of the coat hanger type is a snap for attaching a sinker.

When the sinker and rig hit bottom, the baits hang out from it either right on the bottom or above it. This allows you to fish two baits at the same level or at different levels. You can also attach a float to hold the spreader rig just off the bottom so both baits suspend there. This arrangement is very good for floating bait when fishing from a pier or bridge. Ⓔ

Chapter 10
Live Bait

Using the natural food that fish eat is often the best way to catch them. Live bait often works when nothing else does, but getting the bait and keeping it alive can be a problem. Learn some live-bait basics and you should catch more and bigger fish.

Kinds of Live Bait

Some fish will eat just about anything that wiggles while others are very specific in their feeding habits. Although you can usually buy most kinds of live bait, catching it yourself is cheaper and guarantees fresh bait. Sometimes getting the bait is almost as much fun as catching the fish, especially if you approach it that way.

Earthworms

Live earthworms are a basic bait for almost all kinds of freshwater fish and even some saltwater species. From a single red wiggler on a hook for bluegill to a gob of them on a hook for mullet, earthworms are an excellent bait. And you can find them in a lot of different kinds, from the small red wigglers to giant night crawlers. Some fish prefer one over the other but almost all fish will hit some kind of earthworm.

FACT

Using the kind of earthworm found near the waters you fish is usually best because they're used to eating them. Rains wash worms into the water so fish there see them often. But at times a different kind of bait can be good. Try big night crawlers even if they don't grow near where you fish. This change can make reluctant fish bite.

Minnows

Many kinds of fish eat smaller fish and you can catch everything from crappie to flounder on minnows. Freshwater shiner minnows are a common species that most fish will readily hit. They're usually small but can grow up to a foot long. Crappie love them when they're about two inches long and a largemouth bass will go crazy over a six- to-eight inch shiner. Some others include fathead minnows, spottail minnows, chubs, suckers, and sculpin.

Small game fish can make good bait, but it is often illegal to use them. Little bluegill are excellent bait for bass, stripers, and catfish, but they can't be used in some places. Check local laws before using any kind of live fish for bait.

Freshwater and Saltwater Baitfish

Baitfish usually travel in schools and game fish will attack them and gorge on them. The most common kinds of baitfish in fresh water are shad and herring. Threadfin shad grow to a few inches long and are a warm-water species. Everything from crappie to catfish will eat them. Gizzard shad get much bigger, can tolerate much colder water, and are good bait for bigger fish.

Blueback herring are a saltwater species that has been trapped in some freshwater lakes during their spawning run and prospered there. Skipjack herring are bigger and have also been trapped in some freshwater lakes. Both are excellent bait for bigger game fish like striped bass and big largemouth bass. Alewives, another kind of small herring, are a popular bait, especially around the Great Lakes.

FACT

Fishermen have introduced into the environment many kinds of exotic species by using them as bait. Never dump unused baitfish into the water at the end of the trip. They may start reproducing and that almost always creates problems for the native fish.

A large number of different kinds of saltwater baitfish make good bait. Menhaden, also called bunker or pogies, in the six-inch range are excellent for almost all kinds of bigger saltwater fish. Blue runner are a type of big open-water baitfish that are used for big-game fish like marlin. All kinds of herring are good in salt water, and mullet make good bait where they can be found. Ballyhoo, needlefish, pinfish, cigar minnows, and others are also good bait in salt water.

Crickets

Crickets and their cousin grasshoppers make good bait for panfish in fresh water. Store-bought crickets are usually brown, which for some reason fish seem to prefer over wild black crickets. Drop a cricket into a bluegill bed and it usually won't have time to settle down before a fish eats it. Crickets can also be used to catch catfish and other species but they're best for bream.

Other Live Bait

Just about any kind of small critter can be used as live bait. Some common ones used in fresh water include:

- Catalpa worms
- Crayfish
- Frogs
- Grub worms
- Hellgrammites
- Leeches
- Mealworms
- Salamanders
- Wasp larvae
- Wax worms

And some popular saltwater baits include:

- Bloodworms
- Clams
- Crabs
- Eels
- Sandworms
- Shrimp
- Squid

Many saltwater baits also work well in fresh water for a variety of fish. Although most won't stay alive in fresh water, they can be fished dead or as cut bait for catfish and other bottom feeders. Eels will live in fresh water and are good bait for stripers, bass, and catfish. The same goes for the baits used mainly in freshwater fishing. They can be used live in salt water if they survive, but can also be used as cut bait or dead bait if they don't.

When to Use Each

Use live bait any time you want to catch fish! Depending on availability and your ability to keep bait alive, it will almost always out-fish any other kinds of baits. There may be some presentations that prohibit the use of live bait, but you can almost always find a way to present live bait to fish. Sometimes it may be slower to fish with live bait than with artificials but slowing down and using live bait will usually pay off in higher numbers of fish caught, as well as bigger fish landed.

Using live bait can create problems. Fish are usually hooked deeper and are harder to release alive when caught on live bait. Live bait like crawfish or minnows may also escape into waters where they are not native and establish populations that cause problems.

Some waters may be fished with artificial bait, only. Check regulations before fishing with live bait to make sure it's legal. Be especially careful on trout steams, because many of them are artificial bait, only.

Live Bait for Fresh Water

Some freshwater fish such as walleye are known to be finicky eaters, so you almost always have to use live bait. A jig may not catch many walleye but tip it with a worm, leech, or minnow and they will bite. Bream and crappie both will hit small jigs and flies but prefer live worms and minnows most of the time.

For trophy bass a big live minnow like a golden shiner is hard to beat. Some guides in Florida specialize in shiner fishing because it produces lunker bass better than anything else. Almost as many big bass are caught on live crayfish, which are good bait for smallmouth and largemouth, too. Drop a crayfish down around a rock reef in the Great Lakes and you can land a trophy smallmouth.

Stripers and hybrids will hit live herring and shiners much better than they'll hit artificial baits. Stripers and catfish love eels. And flathead catfish prefer live minnows to any other bait. Even the pickiest trout will readily eat a hellgrammite.

Yellow perch will hit wax worms and mealworms under the ice when they ignore everything else. Trout can be taken on worms and crickets better than on artificial flies and spinners. And the traditional baits for bream are earthworms and crickets.

Options for Saltwater Live Bait

All kinds of saltwater flats fish, including trout and redfish, love shrimp. A live menhaden or mullet will get a trophy tarpon to bite when all else fails. Flounder seem to prefer a live minnow drifted near the bottom to just about any other kind of bait. And surf fishermen catch everything from sea bass to sharks on live minnows.

FACT

You'll get more bites if you match the size of your bait to the fish you're after. For fish with small mouths, use smaller bait. And try to match the size of the bait to what the fish normally feed on. This is known as "matching the hatch."

Saltwater stripers love eels just as much as their landlocked freshwater counterparts. Dropping a live squid or minnow to the bottom on a reef will quickly attract the attention of grouper, sea bass, and all the other predators around it. Trolling live bait for big-game fish like sailfish, marlin, and swordfish is the best way to take them. Bluefish eat up whole bloodworms, and croaker and spots in bays eat them up when the worms are cut into bite-size pieces.

How to Keep Bait Alive

Special containers are made for most kinds of live bait, and you should use the right one. Most live bait does better if kept cool and out of the sun. Storing live bait for long periods of time is a lot of trouble so plan on using your bait soon after getting it. It's much better to get fresh live bait for each trip rather than to get a lot and try to keep it for a several days.

Keeping Freshwater Bait Alive

Live earthworms in the refrigerator may not sound too appetizing, but a cool, moist place is the best place to store them. Put the paper cups they're sold in into the refrigerator and they'll last several days. If you dig your own earthworms, put them in a paper cup with a lid—don't use plastic or metal. Paper will allow the soil to breath and not condense too much moisture in it.

Minnows can be kept in an aerated tank or a thirty-gallon plastic trashcan. Put an aquarium aerator in the bottom of the trashcan and the minnows will keep for several weeks. Drop a little goldfish food on top of the water if you plan on keeping them more than a few days. Take a few minnows out to use and leave the rest for later. If you're staying at the lake or have a pond nearby, you can use a minnow bucket with holes in it to let fresh water flow through.

ESSENTIAL

> On hot days add a few ice cubes to your minnow bucket to cool the water. Do this all during the day to keep them lively and healthy. Don't add many at one time; if you get the water too cool, they'll die when you put them into the warmer water you're fishing.

Crickets will live a long time in a good wire cricket box. Put a cut potato in the box with them each day for moisture and food. Make sure the box is in the shade, out of direct sunlight. A cricket box with a wide top and a metal sleeve allows you to take out one cricket at a time. You can use it while fishing and to keep them alive between trips. A wire tube with a stopper in one funnel-shaped end also works well, but it's more trouble to get a cricket out when you need it.

For other baitfish, a round bait tank is just about the only way to keep them alive unless you have a dock on the lake and can put a big wire basket in the water for them. While you're fishing from a boat, you can keep them in a bait tank or a thirty-gallon plastic trashcan, but you need to use a twelve-volt aerator or small bilge pump to keep the water circulating. Since most baitfish are open-water fish they need a big tank, and won't survive well in smaller minnow buckets.

Mealworms, wax worms, and grubs kept in a container of meal in the refrigerator will stay alive and healthy for several days. Leeches, salamanders, and hellgrammites can be kept in moist moss in a tightly sealed container with a few air holes. Crayfish need to have shallow containers of water that stays aerated. Wasp nests containing larvae need to be put in a paper sack and kept in the refrigerator, but be real careful when you open it because some may have matured and can sting you.

ALERT!

Make sure everyone in the house knows where you keep your bait in the refrigerator. Don't take a chance that a kid may open a bag with a live wasp in it, or that anyone may open the wrong container looking for a snack.

Keeping Saltwater Bait Alive

Saltwater bait is much harder to keep live and healthy than freshwater bait. Eels can be kept in baskets in the water but unless you have a place on the water to keep them, it's hard to manage. Most saltwater baitfish can be kept for a day of fishing in a freshwater bait tank or in the built-in bait tank on a boat, but most will not last more than a day or so. Shrimp and squid can also be kept in a well-aerated bait tank for a day or so, but you need a tank with fresh saltwater pumping into it to keep them alive for any length of time.

Sandworms and bloodworms will stay alive in the moss they're packed in if you keep them moist and cool. Refrigerate them just like earthworms and make sure they're in paper cartons that can breath; however, it's best to start with fresh ones every day. If you keep any leftovers for use later, don't depend on them.

How to Hook Live Bait

How you put a live bait on the hook can make a big difference in how long it stays alive, how it moves, and how easy it is to hook a fish when one bites. Minnows and baitfish can be hooked in several different ways, as can earthworms. Leeches, crayfish, and crickets are best hooked just one way. Always try to put the hook through just enough of the bait to hold it without killing it or impeding its action. For the best results using live bait, learn the best way to put it on the hook.

Hooking Freshwater Bait

An earthworm can be hooked in the middle with both ends dangling or hooked near one end so it stretches out its full length. In either case it's best to run the point of the hook all the way through the worm's body and then back through so part of the worm rests on the crook of the hook. This will hold it better and keep it from tearing off as easily.

When putting on a gob of worms hook several in the middle so you have many wiggling ends. With big night crawlers, stick the hook into the worm about an inch from one end and run the point inside the worm down and come out an inch or so below the entry point. That will make two ends that dangle some and hide the hook inside. You can also leave the hook inside the worm to keep the hook from snagging weeds, but since earthworms are so soft, the hook will penetrate them easily.

Hook crickets under the collar behind their head, sticking the hook in under one side and bringing it out the other, being careful to keep the hook near the surface. Hook leeches through the sucker by sticking the hook through one side and out the other. Salamanders can be hooked through the lips, and frogs through one foot, allowing them to swim.

With crayfish, hook them through the tail with a light wire hook. Grub worms, wasp larvae, wax worms, and mealworms are best hooked by running the hook through their body one time. Sometimes putting a gob of the smaller worms on the hook works best.

Minnows can be hooked though the lips or eyes; hooking them up front is best when trolling with them. When hooking them through the lips, start the hook below the mouth and run the hook back far enough to get some of the hard nose gristle in the hook crook for better holding power. When tail hooking minnows or baitfish, hook them up near the dorsal fin and they'll try to swim down against the pull of the hook. Hook them near the tail and they'll try to swim up. In both cases keep the hook near the surface, getting just enough meat in the hook to hold without getting near the backbone.

Putting Saltwater Bait on the Hook

For fishing an eel, hook it through the lips. You'll need a rag to hold these slimy bait to get a hook in them. Run a sharp hook through the back of a small crab's shell or though one side just behind the claw arm for different actions. You may want to pinch off the claws on fiddler crabs and others to make them more appetizing to the fish and easier for you to handle.

Hook minnows and baitfish for saltwater fishing the same way as for freshwater fishing. Always use a hook with a big enough gap so it doesn't pinch the body of the minnow or baitfish when hooking them in the back. You want them to be able to swim and move freely. Fishing minnows without weight and hooked so they either swim up or down works well around offshore oil rigs.

FACT

If you handle live bait gently it will last longer and be more active, resulting in more bites. Make sure you don't injure the bait more than absolutely necessary when hooking it. Don't squeeze too tight when putting the hook in.

Catching Your Own Live Bait

Collecting you own live bait can be a lot of fun and usually a lot cheaper then buying it. By catching it yourself you make sure it is fresh and handled in ways that guarantee it will be more lively. You may need to make an initial investment in a net or trap, but you can use both for many years. Some baitfish can even be caught on rod and reel and put up a good fight just like the game fish you're hoping to catch with them.

How to Catch Freshwater Bait

Digging earthworms is a rite of passage for most kids. All you need is a small trowel, a bucket, and some moist, rich soil. Dig carefully and turn over piles of dirt to find them. Raking leaves around in the woods will uncover swamp crawlers and night crawlers and all you have to do is pick them up. And you can go out after a rain at night with a flashlight and pick up night crawlers off your lawn if you live in the right areas.

Traps work well for crayfish, minnows, and eels. Bait up the traps and leave them in shallow water overnight for a good supply of bait. You can buy traps or make a simple basket out of screen wire or hardware cloth, with a funnel-shaped opening pointing inside at one end. Eel pots set in rivers will collect eels for later use.

A small net with a long handle is good for collecting frogs and small minnows one at a time in shallow water. Turn over rocks in streams or rivers for crayfish, salamanders, and hellgrammites, and catch them in a small net or your hands. A net will also help you catch crickets or grasshoppers in fields, or you can just grab them with your hands. Cast nets and seines work well in fresh water. Throw the cast net over schools of herring or shad and use a seine in the shallows to catch minnows, crayfish, and grass shrimp.

ESSENTIAL

A cast net is a round net with sinkers around the edge and a rope through the middle. The rope pulls cords to draw the net closed after you throw it and it sinks, trapping fish it goes over. A seine is a long net with small mesh that has a stick at each end for a person to hold while pulling it through the water to catch fish. Read more about nets in Chapter 15.

Use a light rod and reel and bait a tiny hook with little dough balls or pieces of worm or shrimp to catch minnows and small bluegill for bait. Shiners will hit dough balls and put up a good fight if they're six inches long or bigger. It helps to bait up an area with meal or fish food to attract schools of minnows, shiners, and little bluegill before fishing for them.

Catching Saltwater Bait

Cast nets work well for mullet, menhaden, and other schooling baitfish. They also work well for shrimp. You can often get dozens of baitfish on one throw of the net. Pulling a long seine on a beach can catch shrimp, minnows, baitfish, and crabs. Although a seine takes two people to pull, it can catch enough bait for a whole trip in just a few minutes.

Traps work well in salt water, too. Baskets and pots will catch minnows, baitfish, crabs, shrimp, and eels if placed in the correct areas. Check them often and empty the bait into a holding tank. This is best done from a boat.

Sabiki rigs are made for catching lots of baitfish quickly. They're rigs made up of tiny flies attached along a line a few feet long. You hook a sinker at the end and jig the line of flies up and down with a rod, and you can often catch several baitfish at a time. It doesn't take long to fill up a bait tank with herring or other small baitfish with one of these rigs.

You can also catch lots of saltwater baitfish on rod and reel. Bait a small hook with pieces of cut bait and fish it in shallow water. Some saltwater baitfish like little pieces of worms, clams, or squid and can put up a good fight when hooked on a light rod and reel. It's legal in some areas to snag baitfish with a weighted treble hook.

QUESTION?

What does it mean to "snag" a fish?
This means the fisherman is simply allowing the hook to catch on to any part of the fish that passes by. It's easy to snag a fish in a large school because at least one fish will pass by close enough to get caught someplace on its body. This is illegal in many states. (Read more about illegal hooks in Chapter 17.)

Buying Live Bait

If you don't want to catch your own bait you can buy it. To make sure it's fresh and lively, buy your bait the day you go fishing, at a bait store close to where you intend to fish. Try to develop a good relationship with the owner of the bait store and you'll get good information along with your bait purchase.

Getting Live Freshwater Bait

Earthworms, crickets, and minnows are a staple of most bait stores. They're fairly easy to keep in big tanks or cages and suppliers usually visit these stores at least weekly. Make sure you purchase enough bait for the day. It's better to have some left over than to run out when the fish are biting.

When buying earthworms, ask to see them. There's usually a box where the container can be dumped so you can see the number as well as the health of the bait you are buying. If buying crickets, look for lively, active crickets that climb on the container. Make sure there are no dead ones in the bottom. Crickets are measured by volume rather than counted and you don't want to pay for a lot of dead ones. With minnows make sure they're swimming actively in the bucket and not lying dead on the bottom. They're usually counted out and sold by the dozen.

You can probably also find wax worms and mealworms in most bait stores, but the other baits may be harder to find. When you get closer to your fishing spot, you're more likely to find baitfish like herring and shad because they can be caught and sold quickly without transporting them long distances. You may find salamanders, frogs, and crawfish, too, but they are not nearly as common.

No matter how you get your bait, invest in a good container of the correct size and type for it. This will ensure better survival of the bait while you're fishing and will save you money in the long run on bait cost.

Finding Live Bait for Salt Water

Bloodworms and sandworms are similar to earthworms in the way they're boxed and sold, so you should make sure you pour them out and check for numbers as well as the health of the bait. Most saltwater bait is sold near the coast at marinas and bait stores near piers and fishing areas. Ask when the bait was caught and delivered since many kinds don't keep well.

Chapter 11

Prepared Bait

It's often more convenient when going fishing to take along bait that's not alive. There are many kinds of baits that fill the gap between live bait and artificial bait; they're easy to carry and easy to use. Some of them were once alive but others are things fish would never see in their natural world.

Frozen Bait

Many kinds of live bait can be frozen and kept for a later time when you can't get live bait. You can often buy frozen bait cheaply, or you can prepare it yourself. You can freeze the right amount for each trip and keep it a long time until needed. Frozen baits also make good chum.

Chum is bait that's put out to attract fish to an area. Pieces of fish and other bait make good chum and you can freeze them whole and grind them up when needed or grind them up and freeze the chum in containers for later use. Chumming isn't legal in all areas though, so you should check with your local authorities first.

Kinds of Frozen Bait

Just about any kind of minnow or baitfish can be frozen and used later. Freezing them does make them soft and they won't stay on the hook as well as when fresh, but they will work. Freeze whole shiners, small shad, and other small fish in cartons to thaw and use later. If possible freeze the fish separately on a cookie sheet then dump them into a container with a tight top. This allows you to take out a whole minnow without chipping apart a chunk of frozen fish or waiting for the whole block to thaw.

FACT

Earthworms don't freeze well at all and you shouldn't bother trying. They're usually fairly easy to find in bait stores, so plan on buying them fresh rather than trying to freeze them.

Bigger baitfish can be frozen whole then cut up after they thaw, or you can cut pieces the size you will use and freeze them like individual minnows. Freezing fish in cartons of water will help them keep in better condition longer but they are harder to use since you have to let the whole block thaw. If you're planning on grinding them up for chum, it doesn't matter whether you freeze them whole or in blocks of ice.

Crayfish can be frozen whole for later use as can frogs, crabs, and salamanders, but they don't work as well when frozen. Clams will work after being frozen and are best if you freeze them in the shell; the shell will open and you can get the meat out easier. Shrimp and squid both freeze well and can be used whole or cut up after thawing. Hellgrammites can be frozen separately and used when thawed, but live ones are better bait.

Crickets, mealworms, wax worms, catalpa worms, and grub worms can all be frozen in a container with corn meal in it. The meal keeps them from sticking together and from becoming mushy when thawed. Catalpa worms are probably the best of the group to use after freezing.

Other soft-bodied baits like sandworms and bloodworms don't freeze well at all. They become mushy after freezing, and the only way you can use them is to put them in net bags. With these and other very mushy baits, cut a small square of net material, such as pantyhose, and wrap the bait it in, tying the top together. Then attach it to the hook inside the net bag. Other baits are better for that purpose. Although they have soft bodies, leeches can be frozen individually and you won't have the problem of them wrapping around the hook as they do when they're fresh. Wasp larvae can be frozen in the nest and used later but they do become softer, and you can't refreeze them.

How to Fish Frozen Bait

Some fish like blue catfish seem to take frozen bait almost as well as live bait. Others such as bass are unlikely to hit bait that's not alive. Flounder and other bottom-feeding saltwater fish will hit frozen bait, and some game fish will hit whole frozen baitfish when trolled or given movement some other way.

Add a small inline spinner in front of your hook to give flash to frozen bait. This will help attract game fish that usually feed on live bait and make frozen bait more appealing.

Since frozen bait often becomes softer, the use of a double or treble hook can help. You don't have to worry about injuring the bait since it is already dead, so use a double or treble hook and stick it into the bait in more than one place. Try to arrange it so it hangs naturally on the hook. You can also use a bait holder rig with two hooks tied together with a short leader. Stick one hook in the head of the frozen bait and the other in the tail to hold it better, or keep it straight in the case of a small frozen minnow.

Frozen bait won't have any action of its own but it works well for bottom feeders that scavenge for food. Rig it on a fish finder rig or a simple sinker and hook, cast it out, and let it sit for catfish in fresh water and grouper in salt water. For fish that prefer a moving bait, drift it on spreader rigs or bait walkers (see Chapter 9 for more on rigs and bait walkers). Tipping a jig with a frozen minnow and casting it will work for walleye and other fish that like movement in their food, too.

Freeze-Dried Bait

You may accidentally freeze-dry baits yourself if you leave some minnows in the freezer too long, but it is better to purchase them. Many kinds of bait ranging from crickets to minnows are freeze-dried and sold in zipper bags. They keep well for a long time and will catch fish, but not as well as fresh-frozen baits. Use them as an emergency supply or when you need lightweight bait.

FACT

Freeze-dried baits are the lightest baits you will find so they're good baits to carry when backpacking. They keep for a long period of time, don't take up much space, and are very lightweight, all of which are important factors when backpacking.

Kinds of Freeze-Dried Bait

Minnows are the most popular kinds of freeze-dried baits and many tackle stores sell them. They're often more expensive than live or frozen bait and don't work as well. You may also find crickets, grasshoppers, crayfish, and leeches for fresh water, and clams, squid, shrimp, and crabs for salt water. Look for baits that are whole, not broken apart, and store them so they won't be damaged after you buy them.

How to Fish Freeze-Dried Bait

It's usually best to soak freeze-dried baits in water to soften them before using. Treble and double hooks hold them better than single hooks, and bait holder hooks (hooks with barbs on the shaft or a small spring) may be a good choice. These baits retain the smell of the live bait so they can be effective for fish like catfish that scavenge for food using smell.

Add a small inline spinner to these baits for added attraction, too. They make good jig tippers and can add enough smell and meat to them to make you get more bites. Fishing them under a cork or sitting still on the bottom will get bites from bluegill and other active feeders that eat any kind of food they can find. The ones for salt water work for bottom feeders when dropped down on a fish finder rig but will work better when drifted under a cork or moved along the bottom.

Preserved Bait

Storing bait in brine or some other preservative can make it last a long time and keep it useful. Some baits, like salmon eggs, have to be preserved or they won't last. You can also find some kinds of preserved baits that fish would otherwise never see, like pork rind. Preserved baits are easy to carry and will last practically forever.

Kinds of Preserved Bait

Pickled minnows and frogs can be found in many tackle stores, covered in the preserving fluid and stored in zipper bags or bottles. They stay moist and keep well, and you can take out one bait at a time and use it without damaging the others. When preserved correctly the baits retain their natural colors, or have color added to them to attract fish.

Crayfish, leeches, crabs, worms, and many other kinds of baits can also be found pickled or preserved in some kind of fluid, too. Since the pickling process adds a smell of its own, these baits can be less effective than frozen or freeze-dried baits. If preserved in brine the saltwater baits will not have an added smell and many freshwater fish, like bass, seem to like salty bait, so it may actually help.

Pork rind—the skin and fat of a hog—is a special bait that is cut into strips or chunks and pickled in brine. It's been around for many years and, except for live bait, may be one of the best big bass baits available. Pork rind is cut into thick strips with fat attached to make eel and worm shapes and into chunks with tails for jig trailers. The thin skin is cut into strips for trailers for spinners and spoons.

You can buy salmon eggs, which are preserved in borax, making them tough enough to stay on an egg holder hook. Eggs would dry out quickly if not preserved and would be so soft they wouldn't stay on the hook. Eggs can also be dyed different colors for an added attraction for fish.

Fish tend to swallow prepared baits, making hook removal difficult. If you're planning on catching and releasing, it's best to avoid baits like salmon eggs, which fish swallow so deeply you can't remove the hook without injuring them.

How to Fish Preserved Bait

The "jig and pig" of bass fishing gets its name from a jig tipped with a pork frog, which is a chunk of pork skin and fat that is pickled in brine. Pickled pork is cut into chunks with tails on them that wave like crayfish arms when fished behind a jig. Pork chunks can be dyed different colors and have been known to catch a huge number of big bass. Although plastic chunks have replaced them in many cases, pork still works best in cold water and gives something extra that plastic can't match.

A small strip of white pork rind added to a small spinner is deadly for bream and other panfish. The little strip waves enticingly as you reel the spinner through the water. Put a long strip behind a spoon and swim it through grass beds and lily pads for pike and bass.

Drifting a salmon egg in a stream is one of the best ways to catch trout. It's a very natural bait that trout naturally feed on and it's hard to beat. And unlike natural eggs, preserved ones can be dyed different colors to show up better in different colored water and to attract fish under a wide variety of conditions. In some trout streams, eggs aren't allowed, so check regulations before using them.

Other pickled and preserved baits are just like frozen baits because they work best for bottom feeders that find their food by scent. You can hook these baits to jigs or put a small spinner ahead of them for added flash to attract fish. And they often stay on the hook well since the pickling process sometimes makes them very tough.

Prepared Specialty Bait

You will often see tubs, tubes, and jars of baits made of a variety of materials that attract different kinds of fish. Blood bait for catfish is one of the most common kinds, but you'll find other similar baits for saltwater and other freshwater fish. All such baits have some kind of fish attractant, like blood, mixed with a material that forms a paste that will hold it together and help it stay on the hook. Some even have special hooks made with plastic tubes to hold the paste on them.

Kinds of Specialty Bait

You can find tubs of dough in various consistencies with a variety of special scents mixed in. You can also make your own dough baits, and some people develop special formulas they guard like top-secret military files. One of the simplest doughs to make is the breakfast cereal Wheaties mixed with strawberry soft drink. You make a small ball of this dough and put it on a hook for carp and catfish.

Blood baits and stink baits for catfish are common, too. They come in tubes, tubs, and jars, and some have natural materials like cheese or blood in them, while others are artificially flavored with everything from garlic to anise oil. Some are so strong you won't want to open them in an enclosed area or put them on a hook without wearing a glove.

Some other baits that fit this category are not really bait at all. Canned peas and whole-kernel corn make good bait for a variety of saltwater fish as well as catfish and carp in fresh water. Bream will hit whole English peas, and trout seem to really like miniature marshmallows. You can also use commercial fish food, which works better than anything else for fish raised in hatcheries and released into the water, because they're used to it. Trout will eat anything that resembles a food pellet if raised on it, and the pellets themselves make good bait.

Cheese baits, which are dough baits with a cheese smell, attract trout when a small ball of it is put on a hook; it may look like a food pellet or a salmon egg to the trout. Other dough baits with all kinds of flavors ranging from garlic to fish attract many kinds of fish in both salt water and fresh water.

How to Fish Specialty Bait

Dough balls are usually fished on the bottom for carp. A small short-shanked hook is best, and you should hide the whole hook in the bait. Make a ball or a egg-shaped pellet and form it around the hook and shank, hiding the whole hook in the bait. Fish it without weight if possible or use a small Split Shot or Egg sinker if you need weight to get it to the bottom and hold it there. Fish it on a tight line and hold on.

FACT

Many people use a rod holder when fishing prepared bait. Placing the rod in a holder keeps the bait still and allows you to use several rods at one time. Make sure the rod is securely attached because a big cat or carp can pull your rod and reel into the water.

Cheese baits and food pellets for trout and other fish can be cast on a light outfit with no weight and drifted with the current for best results. Make a ball on the hook and cover it as much as possible. If the current is too strong to fish without weight, add a Split Shot and fish it under a cork.

Be sure to check out the hooks made for these baits. Some have teardrop-shaped plastic holder covering a treble hook. You squeeze the bait into a slot in the holder and it slowly dissolves in the water, attracting the fish. Some hooks have a metal spring around the shank that helps hold the bait on the hook. You need some kind of special hook for the softer paste baits, especially the ones that come in tubes.

Fresh-Meat Bait

Fresh-meat baits are parts of animals that are used to fish catfish or sharks. Although they wouldn't normally find these baits in their natural environment, the baits work well for these fish. These baits can be frozen but are best when fresh. They usually leave a blood trail in the water to attract the fish.

Kinds of Fresh-Meat Bait

Chicken parts are a staple of cat fishing. Livers, gizzards, hearts, and even pieces of chicken meat can be used. Liver is the traditional bait and catches many catfish each year. Chunks of bloody meat from cows, goats, and pigs can be used for shark fishing, as well as for catching some bottom-feeding saltwater fish. Livers, lungs, hearts, and other internal organs from those animals can also be used.

How to Fish Fresh-Meat Bait

Chicken liver is soft and doesn't stay on the hook very well. If it's fresh it will stay on a treble hook well enough, but after being frozen it gets very mushy. Cut a small square from old pantyhose and make a small bag for the thawed liver and tie the top shut. You can then hook this bag of liver on a single hook and fish it on the bottom for catfish, just like fresh liver.

With chicken gizzards, animal livers and hearts, and other tough organs you can cut a small piece and put it on the hook. A one-inch square piece of beef liver is about the right size for catfish when used on a #1 hook and fished near the bottom of a lake or stream. A chunk of meat the size of a softball on a 10/0 hook might be more appropriate for a shark off the coast.

Dead-Fish Bait

Cut-up parts of fish probably deserves a special category. Any kind of fish can be used and is a natural food for many species of game fish. You can adjust the size of the bait easily, and it is inexpensive because you can catch your own or cut a lot of pieces of bait from one bigger bought fish.

Kinds of Dead-Fish Baits

Any kind of bloody or oily fish makes good cut bait for catfish, stripers, and most saltwater fish. Bigger baitfish can be cut into smaller parts for smaller fish or to make it bait more hooks. You can also cut large fish into chunks to make it the right size for the fish you want to catch and also to make it go further. One reason cut bait works so well is it releases the scent of the fish into the water better.

Keep a sharp knife and cutting board with your fishing tackle and make cut bait anytime you want to use it. You can chop up a fish you catch or cut up one you brought along. A bigger fish is easier to handle and carry if you keep it whole until you need to cut it up later.

How to Fish Dead-Fish Bait

A mullet can be purchased cheaply in most grocery stores and cut into quarter-size pieces for catfish bait. Those pieces make good bait for still-fishing with rod and reel and also for baiting trotline and other set hooks. A six-inch gizzard shad or blueback herring can be cut in half and each half used to catch stripers, hybrid, and catfish. Troll with the tail section or fish it on the bottom on a fish finder rig for both species.

Chop menhaden in half for a bite-size bait for smaller saltwater cats, grouper, and other bottom-feeding fish. For big fish like sharks you might need to cut a ten-pound fish in half and use each half for bait. Cutting it releases blood and oil into the water to attract the sharks. Suspend big baits under a big cork or even use a balloon to keep it at the right depth for the fish you're after.

It's easy to cut fish into pieces on the spot for whatever purpose you need at the moment. Cut a long thin strip for more action and less drag in moving water. Cut a chunk with several skin tails for even more action. A cube might work best for bottom-fishing while a long teardrop shape will cast and retrieve better. Experiment with different shapes and sizes to see what works best.

Attractant Additives and Dyes

Over the years fishermen have dipped their bait into attractants to improve the bite. Bass fishermen have used everything from anise oil to blood, and saltwater fishermen have used blood, chum, and other mixtures to add smell to their baits. As a result, a big commercial industry has developed, and now some companies produce nothing but attractants. You can still make your own or buy a wide variety of products. You can also buy products that dye your bait and lures, and some of those also add smell.

Kinds of Additives and Dyes

There's just about any kind of additive you could possibly want on the market. One company, Jack's Juice, produces the following spray-on additives:

- Clam scent
- Crab scent
- Crawfish scent
- Garlic scent
- Lizard scent
- Menhaden oil
- Salty shad scent
- Shrimp scent

All these additives are put on live bait and lures to make them more attractive to fish. Other companies offer other scents so there's a wide range to choose from. No matter what kind of fish you're after in both salt and fresh water, there's a scent available to attract them.

How to Use Additives and Dyes

Spray your bait with the attractant or dip your bait into it. Refresh the attractant every few casts because it wears off. When using garlic or other strong scents, you can smell them and know when they need refreshing. These attractants can be used with any kind of live bait or lure.

ALERT!

Many kinds of spray-on scents will stain you and your boat; it will stick to skin, carpet, and fiberglass and leave a smell and dark stain. Unless you want to smell the scent from now on, make sure you hold the bait or lure over the side of the boat while spraying on the additive.

Mix the attractants with prepared specialty baits like dough or blood baits. Or you can make your own special mix by using some of the commercial attractants and anything else you choose. You might find a green dough ball that smells like garlic is just the bait carp in your favorite lake are waiting for.

With the dyes, dip the bait into it and leave it until it changes color. You can even buy special bedding for earthworms that makes them turn different colors. There are many dyes for plastic worms, and for some kinds of live bait.

Chapter 12

Artificial Bait

Artificial baits range from soft-plastic minnows that look like they could swim to garish spinners that look like nothing that has ever swum. A wide variety of fish will hit artificial baits, which are very popular in both saltwater and freshwater fishing. They're easy to keep and use, and they don't die on you or make a mess.

Plugs

Hard plastic or wood baits are designed to attract the fish's attention and get them to try to eat it. They can come in sizes ranging from tiny one-eighth ounce baits to huge baits weighing several ounces. All are designed to look like food and most have two or three sets of treble hooks on them. You give them action by casting or trolling and they will cover the water from the surface to many feet deep.

Floater-Divers

Plugs that float at rest but dart under the surface when moved are very popular for game fish ranging from bass to bluefish. They have a small lip near the head that makes them go under when they are pulled in the water. Most dive a few inches to a couple of feet, and by pulling them under and letting them float back up they look like hurt baitfish, an easy meal for a predator.

Most floater-diver plugs are long and thin and wobble from side to side when pulled. The action can range from a tight wiggle to a wide wobble and these plugs can be reeled or trolled just under the surface. They can be fished in very shallow water or reeled over underwater weed beds that come near the surface. They're also very effective around any kind of freshwater shoreline cover, or in salt water around offshore structures like oil rigs.

Natural colors, like silver or gold sides with dark backs and lighter bellies, imitate the color of baitfish and are good choices. Sometimes a very bright color like chartreuse or florescent orange will attract attention better in stained water or offer the fish something they don't see every day. You should start with a few natural colors in different sizes but add a couple of bright colors, especially if local fishermen say they're good.

FACT

Some colors of artificial baits may be very popular in a particular area and produce well there but not be as effective in other places. When traveling or fishing new waters, check with local tackle stores to see what's popular before buying plugs to use in that area.

Deep Divers

Although most deep divers float at rest, they have big lips that make them dive deep when reeled in. They're designed to dive to a particular depth and run there, so you can choose one to fish just over a weed bed six-feet deep, or another to bump the bottom in fourteen feet of water. This is important when the fish are holding at a particular depth, too, because you can run the bait right in front of them where they're holding.

FIGURE 12-1

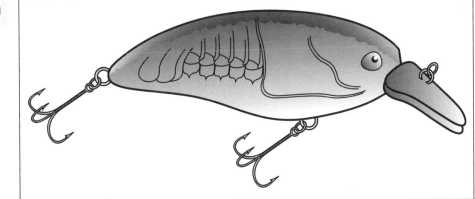

▲ A lipped crankbait.

Deep-diving crankbaits are very popular in bass fishing, and most tackle stores will have hundreds on display in a lot of different sizes, styles, and colors. Some will be painted to look like fish and others will be in bright colors never seen underwater. All will work at different times and in different places. Start by buying a few in natural colors that dive to different depths and add others as you need them.

You can buy one style of plug in several sizes that will cover different depths of water. Shadraps by Rapala come in sizes ranging from #5 to #9, and each size will run a different depth. Purchase a couple of basic colors in each size and you can cover different depths easily.

Deep divers come in a lot of different shapes and their shape controls their action to some extent. Usually fat round plugs have a wider wobble than thin flat plugs but the lip of the plug is more important. Wider lips usually mean wider wobbles. The size of the lip also controls the depth the plug runs. Plugs will small lips run shallower and those with big lips dig deeper.

Lipless Crankbaits

Lipless crankbaits are flat or teardrop shaped and are designed to wiggle when reeled in. They usually sink at rest and have a tight wiggle. Many have a lot of rattles in them to make a lot of noise as they come through the water. They can be fished at any depth depending on the speed you retrieve them and they can even be jigged off the bottom.

ALERT!

Although crankbaits have multiple treble hooks that look like they would securely hold any fish that hits, they are notorious for having fish come off them. Good sharp hooks are extremely important when fishing any kind of plug, so sharpen them often.

Some plugs of this design are made of lead or other metal that sinks fast. These must be reeled very fast to keep them near the surface but they're very effective when fishing deep water. You can either let them sink to the bottom and hop them along it, or let them sink to the depth the fish are holding and work them back at that depth.

Soft-Plastic Bait

Soft-plastic baits come in so many sizes, shapes, and colors it can boggle the mind. The shape is limited only by the imagination of the person making the mold and there seems to be no limits on the colors that can be produced. Many look like minnows or worms that fish are used to feeding on, and others look like creatures from outer space. At one time or another fish will hit them all.

Minnow Imitations

There are a lot of soft-plastic baits shaped and colored just like minnows and baitfish. They're designed to be fished weightless or on a jig head and imitate feeding or injured minnows. Some have swimming tails that twist in the water and others have straight tails that make them dart when fished weightless. Smaller sizes are good in fresh water for everything that eats minnows from bass and crappie to stripers and walleye. They can be fished at any depth with any action you want to give them.

In saltwater fishing, big soft-plastic minnows work well for a wide variety of fish. They can be trolled or jigged on the bottom on a jig head. Plastic lures made of surgical tubing with a chain in it works well when trolled for big-game fish. Minnow and baitfish imitations can be used in many applications because they will attract bites from any species that feeds on live minnows.

Worms and Lizards

In fresh water, plastic worms and lizards catch many bass every year. They're probably the most popular bait and can be fished in a lot of different ways. You can find any size you want from two-inch miniworms to giant twelve-inch lizards and eighteen-inch snakes. Some have scent and salt added to make them more attractive.

The number of colors available makes it impossible to carry them all in your boat, much less in your tackle box. Not only are there solid colors but many have metal flakes in them of varying colors, and there are also two- and three-color worms and lizards. Solid colors with a different color tail are very common.

FACT

The Zoom Bait Company offers sixty different colors in its six-inch lizard, which is just one of more than twenty different types of soft-plastic baits it makes. The number of combinations in soft-plastic baits gets overwhelming very fast. It's best to pick a few colors and stick with them.

Craws, Tubes, and Creature Baits

Soft-plastic baits shaped like crawfish are common and are used as trailers on jigs and also used on Texas and Carolina rigs. Some are very realistic looking and others look like a caricature of a real crawfish. Bass don't seem to mind if they're not perfect. Crawfish imitations work well for bass because the real thing is one of their favorite foods. Tube baits are hollow tube-shaped plastic baits with tentacles on them. When fished on a jig head inside the tube they fall with a spiraling motion. Hopped or crawled along the bottom they look like feeding minnows or crawfish. Small two- to four-inch tube baits are usually fished on light line in clear water, but giant tubes up to eight inches work well for bass when flipped around shoreline cover.

Creature baits have been very popular for bass fishing and they come in a wide variety of shapes and sizes. Some look like lizards with wings and extra legs. Some look like nothing ever alive. All create motion in the water and must look like food to bass because they're very effective baits when fished on Texas and Carolina rigs.

Spinners

The flash of a revolving piece of metal has long been known to attract many kinds of fish. Some spinners come with artificial attachments that look like food, some are made with a bare hook to attach some kind of bait, some are straight, and some are different shapes. They all work better when moving so they can be cast, trolled, or drifted. Colors vary as do size and composition. Every tackle box should have a variety of spinners in it.

Inline Spinners

Inline spinners have a blade spinning around a straight shaft. At one end of the shaft is an eye to tie your line to, at the other is a hook. Some spinners have plastic or metal bodies attached to them that look like fish, and others have nondescript bodies that are added just for weight. Small inline spinners are good for panfish, and big ones will catch anything in fresh or salt water. Huge inline spinners called *bucktails* are made for muskie fishing and are bigger than most panfish you catch to eat.

FIGURE 12-2

▲ An inline spinner.

The hooks on a small inline spinner are usually dressed with hair or feathers that give the bait more action. Big inline spinners for bass may have a single hook with nothing on it. You can add pork chunks or other plastic trailers for more attraction. Inline spinners turn at very slow speeds so they can be fished for inactive fish that don't chase a bait very far.

ALERT!

Inline spinners are known for their ability to twist line badly. Add a small ball-bearing swivel ahead of the inline spinner to avoid line twist. Also look for an inline spinner with a body that has a keel to keep it in one position so it won't twist your line as badly.

You can also buy Snelled hooks with a small spinner on the line above the hook. These rigs are excellent for fishing frozen or other dead bait. The small spinner gives flash and movement while the bait adds scent, flavor, and bulk. They work well when cast or drifted for fish like flounder.

Safety Pin Spinners

Safety pin spinners get their name because they look something like an open safety pin. They're V-shaped with a hook at one end of the V, a spinning blade at the other end, and a line tie in the middle. They're very popular for bass fishing but work well for different species from pike to perch in fresh water.

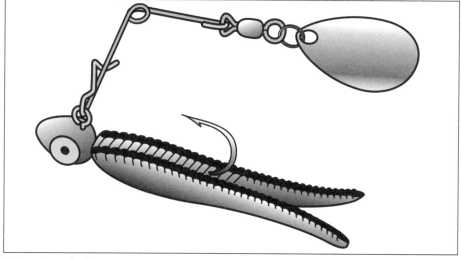

▲ A spinnerbait.

Most spinnerbaits come with a rubber skirt around the hook, and many people add a curly or straight-tailed plastic jig to give it more action. As the spinner is reeled along, the blade or blades revolve giving it flash and vibration. The body with the rubber skirt and the plastic jig trail just below the blades, offering the fish something to hit. Spinners of this type come in different sizes to cover any depth of water.

Tailspinners

Tailspinners are usually small heavy lures with compact teardrop-shaped lead bodies. A little spinner is attached to the tail of the lure to give it flash and vibration to attract the fish; a line tie is on top and a treble hook trails off the bottom. These baits are great for jigging off the bottom. The heavy body gets them down deep fast where they're easy to work.

Another version of the tailspinner is a jig head with a small spinner on the opposite side from the line tie. These baits usually have a single hook dressed with hair or a plastic body and they can be fished near the bottom easily. They attract all kinds of fish looking for a meal of a small baitfish or minnow swimming near the bottom.

Top-Water Bait

Most top-water baits float on the surface and are given action by the fisherman. They look like small struggling bugs, frogs, or injured baitfish trying to swim away. These baits have a variety of actions from popping and chugging in the water to churning it with spinners. Top-water baits offer heart-stopping action when a fish smashes them where you can see and hear the strike. Many kinds of fish in fresh and salt water will hit top-water lures.

Chuggers and Poppers

Baits that chug and pop have a concave face and float on top of the water. When you pull the line they gurgle, pop, and chug in the water. You can work them slow with little gurgles like a dying critter that's an easy meal, or you can work them fast, jerking your rod tip and making them chug along like a fish chasing bait. Both actions will draw viscous strikes from any kind of fish that feeds on smaller fish or other creatures.

Throw a popper beside a stump in a pond, let it settle for a few seconds, then twitch your rod tip to make it gurgle. Hang on! That's when a bass is likely to smash it. Throw a pencil popper near a school of bluefish and jerk it hard and fast. It usually won't go far before a blue tries to jerk the rod out of your hand. In both cases you're attracting the fish with action on top, and when they come to check it out they see something that looks like an easy meal.

FACT

Most top-water plugs have light bellies and dark backs. Often they have some kind of pattern on the back but that's not what the fish sees. The bottom of the plug is usually the only part the fish sees so the top color is more for the fisherman.

Prop Lures

Some top-water plugs have a propeller type spinner on one or both ends of a cigar-shaped body. When you twitch them they churn the water and make a swishing sound, which attracts the fish. If you use a plug with the spinner up front, tie the line in front of the spinner so it doesn't interfere with the action.

These plugs can be an inch or so long with one tail spinner, or up to several inches long with spinners on both ends. The baits with one tail spinner tend to sit with the tail down in the water so the spinner gets a good bite. Those with a spinner on each end tend to float flat so both spinners can work. Plugs with spinners seem to work better in calm water.

A different kind of spinner top-water bait is a buzz bait. It looks like a spinner bait but has a big wedge-shaped blade that is cupped on the ends. When you reel it the bait comes to the surface and churns along, leaving a trail of bubbles. It's one of the few top-water baits that sink at rest. Buzz baits must be reeled constantly to make them work right. A flat head helps keep them on top and you want to move them as slowly as possible while keeping them on top and moving.

Darters

Darters are hard cigar-shaped plugs that float at rest. They have no action at all if you just reel them in, so you must jerk the rod tip to make them move. It takes some practice but you can learn to "walk the dog" with these plugs. When you jerk the bait the nose darts to one side. When you jerk it again it darts the other way. With practice you can make the plug jump from side to side without moving forward much.

ESSENTIAL

To walk the dog with a top-water darter plug you must fish it on a slack line. Leave some slack in the line and jerk the bait, then immediately move your rod tip back toward the bait to give it slack so it can move.

These baits are excellent for big bass and for fishing open water. If blueback herring are present in a lake, darters will catch fish consistently because they make a sound and have action like bass chasing schooling blueback herring on the surface. Although some of the darters are small, most are up to seven inches long.

What knot should I use with top-water plugs?
A loop knot is best on all top water plugs. It allows them to move and have better action. If you don't use a loop knot, use a split ring or snap with them.

Spoons

Spoons were probably some of the first artificial baits. They're either stamped out of solid steel or made by pouring lead into a mold. Choose the right kind and they're effective from the surface to the bottom no matter how deep the water. They can be fished in a variety of ways to catch any kind of fish that feeds on minnows or baitfish.

Casting Spoons

Casting spoons are made of thin metal and look like the bowl of a dinner spoon. They have a hole in one end to tie your line to, and a hook at the other. When you cast them out and reel them in they swim with a wobbling motion. Silver and gold ones flash just like a minnow swimming along. They also come in bright colors that attract fish under varying conditions.

FIGURE 12-4

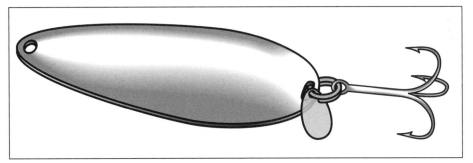

▲ A spoon.

Casting spoons come in a variety of shapes from long and thin to short and wide. They can be a tiny one-inch spoon used for panfish to a nearly foot-long spoon for muskie and saltwater fish. Some have hair or feathers on them to give them added attraction. You can also add a trailer, like a pork rind strip, to the hook for more swimming motion.

Jigging Spoons

Jigging spoons are solid metal, often lead, and come in many shapes and colors They're designed to sink fast and be jigged up and down off the bottom. They will wobble or dart from side to side as they fall but are hard to cast and reel in over shallow water because they're so compact and heavy.

Jigging a spoon up and down near the bottom of a freshwater lake or saltwater reef will attract all kinds of fish. The motion looks like a hurt minnow trying to swim up but drifting back to the bottom because it's hurt. All predator fish love an easy meal like these spoons represent.

When a jigging spoon gets hung on the bottom you can use its weight to knock it loose. Jig your rod tip up and down just enough to raise the end of the spoon and then drop it back. This will knock the hooks lose from most hang-ups.

Jigs

Jigs are usually made by forming a lead head near the eye of a hook that is bent at a ninety-degree angle to the shaft. The hook can be covered with a variety of things to imitate something fish would like to eat. Jigs are some of the simplest artificial baits made and also some of the most effective. They will catch almost any fish that swims

Bucktails

Jigs with hair bodies tied to the shaft of the hook are usually called bucktails because they're often made of deer hair. They can be as small or as big as needed for the kind of fish you're going after, and the weight can vary for any depth you need to fish. The hair can be dyed any color or combinations of colors desired. Small bucktails are good for panfish and huge ones will catch big-game fish in salt water.

FACT

Bucktails are included in survival kits for military pilots to help pilots find food no matter where they might be in an emergency situation. Bucktails are simple to use and effective under a wide variety of conditions.

Rubber Skirts

Jigs with rubber skirts are common in bass fishing. The rubber allows the jig to sink faster than similar-sized hair jigs, and it waves enticingly in the water. Some rubber jigs are grub shaped and others are fish shaped; some have a swimming tail, others a flat tail. All of them can be hopped along the bottom like hurt or feeding baitfish or like crawfish, or they can be reeled along with a steady movement to look like a moving baitfish.

Flies

Lures for fly-fishing come in a variety of styles and types. They're all made to look like food for different kinds of fish. Flies used for trout fishing may be tiny things that resemble a gnat, while those for saltwater fishing may be bigger than the trout you normally catch. All are tied directly to the hook and are very light since you cast the line while fly-fishing, not the lure.

Types of flies include the following:

- **Dry flies:** Floating flies that imitate adult insects
- **Nymphs:** Underwater flies that imitate immature insects
- **Popping bugs:** Floating flies that act like anything from frogs to hurt minnows
- **Streamers:** Flies that look like minnows swimming in the water
- **Wet flies:** Flies that have wings so they look like adult insects underwater

You can buy flies from many sources but many fly-fishermen tie their own for added satisfaction when catching fish. Flies are made from everything from deer hair to bird feathers, and fishermen take great care in tying them so they look like the real thing.

Each kind of fly is fished in a different way. Most dry flies, wet flies, and nymphs are used for trout, while popping bugs are good for bluegill, bass, and some schooling fish in salt and fresh water. Streamers are popular in fresh and salt water and will catch anything from crappie to marlin. Most big-game saltwater fish caught on a fly rod are taken on some kind of streamer. Fishing with flies requires special rods and reels and a good bit of skill. (E)

Chapter 13

Where to Fish

There are many places to fish in both salt water and fresh water; however, the beginner fisherman will probably have to do a little checking to find them. Many are free but some will cost you a few dollars a day. Knowing where to look will help you find a place where you'll enjoy your new-found sport of fishing.

On the Bank

Fishing from the bank is always worth checking out. It can provide excellent fishing and is usually free. Some areas aren't suitable because the water's too deep or the bank is unsafe, but many bank access spots are good for various kinds of fish. You can walk the bank and cast or put a couple of rods out in holders and just sit back and relax.

Freshwater Beaches

Beaches in fresh water are easy to access but sometimes the presence of swimmers prevents fishing on them. But many beaches are in picnic areas that also have spots to fish on the shore away from the swimmers. The best times to check out beaches are during cold weather, at night, or on weekdays when the beaches aren't crowded.

FACT

Some beaches don't allow fishing at all and others are closed at night and during bad swimming weather. Check local regulations and follow the rules. It may be possible to get permission from beach supervisors to fish at specific times.

Boat ramps are usually located on deep water with riprap (rocks placed on the bank to prevent erosion) around them, which can make them excellent fishing spots. There is usually enough area to the sides of the ramp for fishing, and you can cast to the dock even if fishing from it is not allowed. Make sure you don't block the ramp and be ready to move out of the way when boaters want to use the ramp to launch their boats. The ramp itself can also be a good place to cast because it offers a hard bottom that drops off fast.

Marinas are excellent fishing areas and some welcome fishermen. Find one selling bait and tackle and you're likely to find one with many spots to fish. Some even have special designated areas for bank fishing with benches, tables, and fire rings. You probably won't be allowed access to the docks with boats moored to them, but fishing the bank between them can be excellent.

Canals are usually public waters and often have walking paths beside them and public access at many spots. In cities and towns, look for city parks near the canal, roads that run parallel to the canal, and street crossings over the canal. Out in the country, look for places where a public road swings near the canal or crosses it. Bicycle or walking paths also give fishermen access to canals outside city limits.

Saltwater Shoreline

Many beaches on salt water are public and fishing is allowed in most areas. You may have to walk to find good spots to fish where rip currents have made holes or washed food the fish like near the beach, but a little exploring can pay off. Stay away from swimmers who were there first but don't worry about them scaring off the fish. Watch for other surf fishermen and ask them if it's okay if you fish near them, especially if they're catching fish.

Boat ramps are hard to find in salt water because many places have mechanical launching, but saltwater ramps offer the same advantages as freshwater ramps. Check for bank access around the parking lot and near the ramp itself. Ramps sometimes have holes dug out by current on either side if them. Drifting a bait across one of the holes beside or at the end of a ramp is a good way to catch many kinds of fish.

Buying your bait at a marina store can be well worth any extra cost because you can get local information and maybe even a place to fish. It's likely to be fresh, too. Try to get acquainted with the people operating the bait store and you can benefit from their knowledge and location.

Some saltwater marinas cater to fishermen just like freshwater ones do. They sell bait and tackle and will offer tips on where to fish and how to catch fish. Many times they will allow you to fish near the boat docks and around the launch areas. Some will also have picnic areas with bank fishing within the marina.

Saltwater canals can be excellent fishing for many kinds of fish. In port cities, boats moving in the canals will stir up baitfish and make predators feed. The canals are often lined with roads and access can be good. Many cities designate specific fishing areas on canals and make sure there is good access for fishermen on them.

Around Bridges

Bridges usually cross rivers and lakes where they are narrow and the water is deep under them. Many have riprap on either bank running out and forming a perfect rocky point. The pilings and shade under them offer good places for fish to hide. And for fishermen there is almost always some kind of access to the water at bridges.

Underneath Freshwater Bridges

The riprap around bridges is usually excellent for bass, crappie, walleye, and other species of fish. You can usually park on the shoulder of the road at the end of the bridge and walk down to the water, fishing the riprap all the way to the bridge span. It may be a long walk to carry your tackle but the shade under a bridge is very welcome in hot weather.

ALERT!

Be extremely careful when walking on riprap. The rocks can turn or be slippery and cause you to fall, and lots of critters like snakes live there, too. Walk carefully and watch where you're stepping.

Not only does the bridge give you shade in the summer, it will protect you from the rain and help block the wind. And it's surprising how much warmth a bridge holds at night after the sun goes down. That can be a nice surprise on a cool night.

Fish the current coming under a bridge. Try to present your bait so it moves with the current just like a baitfish would move. That's what the local fish are expecting so offer it to them. Cast upstream and let your bait float back weightless or under a cork. Also cast to the pilings of the bridge if you can reach them and let your bait float down by them.

Watch the wind and fish the riprap when the wind is blowing into it. The wind moves plankton to the rocks and the baitfish follow it. The fish you want to catch come in to eat the baitfish. The waves also stir up crayfish and minnows giving game fish more reasons to be there. Try to stand near the water and cast parallel to the rocks, working different depths until you find where the fish are feeding.

On and Under Saltwater Bridges

Saltwater bridges offer the same good fishing you can find in fresh water but there's usually less riprap. Fish under the bridges and near any riprap the same way you would fish these in fresh water. Many saltwater bridges do have walkways for fishing, and you can walk out and fish anywhere along the bridge, trying different spots until you find where the fish are feeding.

If you're allowed to fish from the bridge, try to find the channel or a sandbar or some other change in the bottom contour to fish. You can also fish the tides, changing sides as the tide changes to get your bait to drift out away from the bridge. Use a spreader rig and a big cork, and drift bait just off the bottom.

You can also use the current to drift your bait back under the bridge to fish around pilings. Just remember the pilings are likely to have barnacles on them that will cut your line. You must keep your line off the piling and reel fish away from it fast.

When fishing from a bridge it is a good idea to take a bridge net with you. This is a round net on a rope that you lower to the surface of the water. You can lead any hooked fish over the net, and then raise it without taking a chance on the hook pulling out or your line breaking. Sometimes there will be a community net available on heavily fished bridges.

You may be able to find an old bridge that has been closed to traffic and turned into a fishing platform. When new bridges are built old ones are often left for people to fish from, or the middle is cut out leaving the ends as fishing piers. These spots can be excellent.

From Piers

Fishing piers can be excellent places to catch fish in both salt and fresh water. They run way off the bank giving you access to deeper water and fish you couldn't reach from the bank. Piers themselves are cover for the fish but additional cover is often added around them. Many piers also have small bait and tackle stores on them so you can get anything you need right there.

FACT

Some piers can be fished for free, but others charge a daily rate. Be sure you know before you go if you will have to pay to fish and be prepared with enough cash. Fees are usually low, and a few dollars a day for good fishing is well worth it.

Freshwater Piers

Piers in fresh water are not as common as they are in salt water, but they can be excellent places to fish when you find them. Usually located on bigger lakes and rivers, fishing piers are usually placed near public picnic areas, campgrounds, or boat ramps. You'll seldom find a bait shack on a freshwater pier but it is likely to be less crowded, too. And freshwater piers are generally smaller then their saltwater counterpart.

On many lakes overseen by the Corps of Engineers, special fishing piers have been constructed to give anglers access to the lake. Most are handicap accessible and some have cleaning stations and restrooms available. The Corps often places brush in the water around the piers to attract more fish to the area.

Piers in Salt Water

Most every town on the coast has constructed a fishing pier. These are often right in town and many tourists can usually be found there trying their luck. Don't hesitate to join them. Watch for locals and try to fish like they do, because they most likely know what works on that pier.

Some piers are very short, especially if they're near a channel; others seem to run out a mile. At times fish migrate by piers making the fishing exceptional, but there are always resident fish around piers for you to catch. Live bait usually works best and you can use the current to drift your bait just like from a bridge.

ALERT!

When casting from piers and other crowded areas, watch behind you. If you're not careful you may hook someone walking past. Make sure you know what's behind you before every cast.

When fishing from a pier you may be high above the water, so it's often best to drop your bait straight down. Fish that live around the pier will be near the pilings looking for a meal, and fish moving through the area are just as likely to swim close to the pier, too. If you're high over the water, use a net to land the fish, otherwise you'll lose many of them.

On Docks

Docks and piers are very similar but docks are more likely to be floating, while piers have pilings holding them up. Docks can be found in both fresh water and salt water but are more common in fresh water. Some are made just for fishing, and some allow fishing although that's not their primary purpose. Docks can give you access to deeper water than you can reach from the bank, just like piers.

Docks in Fresh Water

If you are lucky there will be a marina or other private business operating a fishing dock near you. These docks are usually fairly large and consist of a covered area with a walkway around the outside and inside. The center of the dock floor is open and you can sit inside and fish through the hole in the floor while protected from the weather. The walkway around the outside gives you a place to fish when it is nice out there.

It will usually cost you a small fee to fish from one of these fish houses but you can be comfortable in all kinds of weather. Protected from the rain, wind, and snow, you can catch fish in comfort—some even have heaters to keep them warm in the colder weather. Most have brush around them to attract fish, and there's usually bait and tackle available, too.

FACT

Many fish docks are lighted at night so you can fish all night long. The lights help you see what you're doing and they also attract baitfish, which will bring in the crappie, bass, hybrids, walleye, and other fish that feed on them.

Many parks have a dock near the campground for campers to tie their boats, and you can usually fish from these. Fishing is sometimes allowed at gas docks at marinas as long as you don't interfere with business. And docks at waterside restaurants and other businesses are sometimes available for fishing. Docks in marinas where boats are moored are usually off limits to fishermen unless you own a boat tied up there. Sometimes you can fish from the walkway going out to the docks. Be sure to check with the marina operator before fishing from any docks.

Saltwater Docks

Marinas in salt water also have docks where boats are stored, and the same rules apply as for freshwater fishing. Fishing from walkways is sometimes permitted and some marinas may even let you fish off the ends of the docks. If you do go out on a dock with boats present be sure to respect the property of others so you'll be allowed to come back.

Restaurant and other waterside business boat docks like tackle stores, bars, and warehouses in salt water are more common than in fresh water, and fishing is often allowed from them. The docks where fishing boats tie up can be good for many species, especially if they clean their catch and dump waste fish from their nets around them. And transient docks where boats are tied for short periods of time for loading or unloading, or for campers at public parks, can be another place to get away from the bank to fish.

Due to the constant current and water level fluctuation in many areas as the tide goes in and out, floating docks do not hold up as well.

Sometimes in estuaries you will find floating docks with walkways to them and you can often fish from them if they're in public areas.

In Tailwaters

Tailwaters are the waters directly below dams, and these can be excellent places to fish. Many kinds of fish run up rivers to spawn and are stopped by the dam, piling them up in a small area in the tailwater. Water coming from the dam also digs deep holes below them, offering fish a place to hold. Some dams have fishing piers on them for access to the tailwaters and others allow bank access.

ALERT!

Water can rise rapidly below dams when power generation is started or water is released for some other reason. Be extremely careful when fishing below dams and watch for rising water. Make sure you can get to safe ground quickly.

Visit dams on lakes near you and check for access below them. Some have piers, some have parks with bank access, and some have paths you can walk down to get to the water. Be careful when going to the water and make sure you're allowed to fish there.

When you fish below dams you will face strong currents so you will need lots of sinkers to get your bait down to the fish. If fishing for bottom-feeding species like catfish, a fish finder rig works well. Try to find eddies to fish because many kinds of fish like to hold in slower water and wait on the current to bring food to them.

Big catfish are often caught below dams and you will need heavy tackle for them. Walleye also hold below dams and feed there, but you need to concentrate on slower water behind wing dams built to slow the current and rocks around them. Striped bass run up rivers to spawn, and you can even catch saltwater stripers if you fish below the last dam on a river. Landlocked stripers and hybrids also run up rivers to dams above lakes.

Smaller dams can also offer good fishing in their tailwaters. Big bream and cats often hold below pond dams if the creek or stream is big enough for them. Bass can also be caught in the creeks below pond dams. Sometimes a pond dam near a public road will give you access to bank fishing near it, but most times these smaller dams are private and you'll have to get permission to fish them.

Many cities and towns have water-supply lakes that are closed to fishing. Check to see if you're allowed to fish below the dams on these lakes since you won't be fishing on the lake itself and won't be affecting the drinking water.

At Dams and Spillways

Not only do dams congregate fish below them in the tailwaters, they attract fish above them in the lake or pond. The current in the spillway is a good place for fish to hold and feed. The deepest water in the pond or lake is usually right at the dam so it holds fish in hot or cold weather close to the bank.

You can usually walk out on the dam on public ponds and lakes. Look for an overflow pipe or other structure sticking out of the water that keeps the water level from getting too high. It's usually right on the old channel and is a good place to fish since the deepest water will be there. It also offers vertical structure that many kinds of fish like to hold around.

The spillway on bigger lakes and ponds will have water flowing through it much of the time. The current created by this flowing water brings fish in near it. If you can walk to the spillway, cast your bait above it and let the current move it back naturally. Be careful around the spillway because the banks are usually steep and the current can knock you off your feet.

From a Boat

A boat is generally the best way to fish bigger bodies of water. It will give you access to places you can't reach from the bank in fresh water and opens up a lot more types of fishing in salt water. A boat is expensive to buy and maintain, but fortunately you've got other options besides buying one.

Fishing from a Boat in Fresh Water

If you buy a boat for fresh water, be sure to get one big enough for the types of water you fish. A canoe can be a good fishing platform for creeks and small ponds but you'll need a much bigger boat for big lakes, particularly the Great Lakes where you need a boat capable of handling very rough water. Don't go overboard in size because a boat that's too big for the waters you fish can create a lot of problems, too.

Many marinas rent boats or you can hire a guide and fish from the guide's boat, although hiring a guide can be expensive. Another possibility is to join a fishing club as a nonboater. Many bass clubs welcome new members even if they don't have much fishing experience. You'll have to pay for gas and oil for the boat but that is a far cheaper than the alternatives.

Posting notes at marinas in your area or on Internet sites is another way to find fishing partners with boats. Many boat owners like to find partners to help share expenses on fishing trips and you can get access to a boat this way. You'll be expected to pay at least half the cost, but if you post that you're willing to pay all expenses, you're more likely to be find someone to fish with.

ALERT!

Be careful finding partners you've never met. Arrange to meet at some public place like a marina and try to visit over a meal to get to know each other a little before going fishing. Talking over the phone helps but it's safer to meet in person in public first.

Saltwater Fishing from a Boat

Owning a boat for saltwater use can be much more expensive than a boat for fresh water because you'll probably need a bigger boat and upkeep is more expensive. Having your own boat, though, is a great way to be able to go fishing any time you want. Consider all options before buying a boat. If you do decide to buy, the cheapest way to get one is to buy a used boat in the fall at the end of fishing season.

FACT

A couple of old sayings will give you warning about buying your own boat. One says the happiest two days in a boat owner's life are the day the boat is bought and the day it's sold. Another says a boat is a hole in the water where you dump your money.

There are few boats to rent on salt water because of the dangers but there are many opportunities to charter boats. For about $100 per person you can often join in with four or five other people and charter a boat for a day's fishing for any kind of saltwater fish in the area. That price also includes use of tackle and bait for the day, so it's not as expensive as it sounds.

A cheaper way to fish is to sign up for a party boat (also called a head boat). These are big boats that take out forty or more fishermen for a half or full day of bottom fishing. The cost is usually less than $50 a day but you'll have to either bring your own tackle or rent it for a small additional price. But you can usually catch enough fish on one of these boats to make the cost worthwhile.

Chapter 14

You Got a Bite

You have purchased your fishing equipment and rigged it right. After finding a place to fish, you get to the water, put the right bait for the kind of fish you want to catch on your hook, and you cast it out. You get a bite. What do you do now?

Watching a Cork Disappear

Fishing bait under a cork is a good way to learn what to do when a fish bites, and watching the cork move as a fish nibbles your bait is exciting. The cork will show you what's going on underwater if you learn to interpret its movements.

Fixed Floats

Clipping a cork to your line is the most common way of fishing with corks. The cork holds your bait at a set depth and it will move with the slightest bite. When the fish takes the hook the cork will usually be pulled under the water. It is a good way to fish for bream, crappie, flounder, and other kinds of fish that usually grab the bait without nibbling on it.

Watch the cork and note any movement at all. When using bait like minnows or crayfish that can move the cork, you can tell what they're doing. If they're moving slowly and steadily but suddenly start frantic movements, you can bet something is close by that they want to get away from. Get ready for a bite when this happens.

With bait that can't move the cork, any slight tremble will indicate something is checking out your bait. Often the first sign you have is when the cork disappears. If you're fishing near the bottom, the cork may not go under but may fall on its side. When fishing a current the cork may just stop moving when a fish takes the bait.

FACT

A round cork will not indicate soft bites as well as a long thin one. A quill-type float will show you the slightest bite and will fall over even if the fish moves the bait a tiny amount. Quill-type floats are excellent for most kinds of smaller fish.

If the cork trembles, watch it. If it moves off steadily, falls over, stops moving in a current or goes under, set the hook. To set the hook, you raise your rod tip quickly to drive the point of the hook into the fish's mouth. For soft-mouthed fish like crappie you don't want to jerk too hard; a slow-taper rod will help. With hard-mouthed fish and when using thick bait, you want to jerk hard to pull the hook through the bait and into the fish's mouth; you need a fast-taper rod for this.

Slip Floats

Slip floats have a hole in the middle where the line slides freely through it. You can use a bead and stopper knot to make the cork stop the bait at a set depth, or you can let the line move through the hole. When using a stopper, fish it just like you would a clip on a cork.

With a slip float the cork is near the bait so there's no problem casting it as there is when the bait is a few feet below a cork. Cast out and let your bait go to the bottom. Watch the float closely. Even though it is not stationary on the line it will move when a fish bites to tell you when to set the hook.

ESSENTIAL

A slip float works well for fish that bite lightly and release the bait if they feel resistance. You can use a slip sinker and a slip float so the line moves freely when fish bite. Carp and catfish both often drop the bait if they feel any resistance.

If you fish your slip float on a tight line with the reel engaged, a fish running off with the bait will pull the cork under. If the reel is not engaged and the line can come off, the cork will still move and sometimes go under just from the weight and resistance of the line in the water. If the cork goes under or if the cork moves steadily with the line running through it, set the hook.

Another benefit of using a slip float is how it raises your hook and bait off the bottom when you reel in. When you start reeling, the cork will make the bait and hook come straight up, moving it away from trash that you could hang up on.

Feeling Fish Bite

If you're fishing a tight line, the line will usually transmit the action to you when fish bite, even if you don't use a cork. Learning how to interpret what you feel through the line and rod will tell you what's going on at the bait end and help you know what to do. There's no real way to practice learning what a fish feels like; you just have to get on the water and experience it.

Feeling the Bite on Live and Prepared Bait

When a fish takes live and prepared bait, it tastes and feels natural to them and they're likely to hold it in their mouths and even swallow it. Some fish will just suddenly show up and start pulling hard on your line, especially when you're fishing for carp with worms or corn. In salt water many fish hit live and prepared bait so hard all you have to do is pull back; there's no decision when to set the hook.

FACT

A fish doesn't have hands and the only way it can hold your bait is in its mouth. If a fish is moving your bait, you can be sure the bait's in the fish's mouth, right where you want it. If the bait is in its mouth the hook should be, too.

If you put your rod in a rod holder, fish will often hook themselves. But it's still smart to take the rod out of the holder and set the hook hard if you're fishing for big fish like monster cats or fish with hard mouths. Even though they pull hard, the hook may not go in far enough to hold, so set it again to make sure.

Keep an eye on your line whenever you're fishing live and prepared bait. If your line moves, that's an indication a fish is hitting your bait. If your line goes tight, set the hook. If it goes slack or moves sideways, set the hook. Don't wait too long or the fish may feel something it doesn't like and spit out your bait before you can hook it.

Another problem with waiting too long to set the hook with live and prepared baits is the fish will swallow it. The hook will be back in its throat or even in its stomach by the time you hook it and impossible to remove without killing the fish. If you're planning to release any fish you catch, don't use live and prepared bait for this reason.

ESSENTIAL

When planning on releasing fish, use a regular steel hook, not a stainless steel one. If the hook is way back in the fish's throat, cut the line and leave it there. The steel hook should rust and give the fish a chance to survive. Use artificial bait to lessen this problem.

Artificial Bait

When fish take artificial baits they may spit them out quickly, so it's best to set the hook as soon as you think a fish is biting. Artificial baits resemble live bait so the fish are not likely to try to nibble on it like they do prepared bait. They are more likely to take the whole thing into their mouths quickly. Set the hook hard as soon as you feel the fish.

With crankbaits it's a good idea to jerk on them every few seconds during a retrieve even if you don't feel a bite. It's hard to believe that a fish can take a plug with two sets of treble hooks into its mouth and spit it out without getting hooked, but it can. Set the hook hard if you feel any resistance or if the plug stops vibrating. That may mean it's in a fish's mouth.

Bass fishing with plastic worms is famous for the difficulty in knowing when to set the hook and doing it effectively. With billfish in saltwater fishing, waiting until they take the bait but not waiting too long is a difficult decision. A good captain can help you learn when to set the hook on billfish.

Fish are more likely to hold on to soft-plastic baits a little longer since they feel more natural, but you should still set the hook as soon as you feel anything different. This applies to all kinds of worms, lizards, soft-jerk baits, and tube baits. Watch your line and if it jumps or moves sideways, set the hook. It doesn't cost much to set the hook, so do it if there is any doubt.

You can't learn what a fish bite feels like off the water but you can learn what nonbites feel like. Rig up a soft-plastic bait and cast it across different surfaces. Moving a plastic grub across a paved driveway will show you what a hard shell bottom feels like. Cast across gravel, rocks, grass, or brush and you can see what you are feeling.

With top-water plugs you can see the bite and, as a result, the biggest problem is setting the hook too fast. Because of the way the fish takes a top-water plug, it's best to wait until you feel the weight of the fish to set the hook. If you set the hook when you see the water moving, but before feeling the fish's weight, you may pull the hook away from the fish before it is in the fish's mouth.

With spinnerbaits, jigs, and other baits that swim in the water, set the hook any time anything feels different. You may feel a hard pull or you may just lose contact with the spinnerbait when the blade stops turning. If your line goes slack when fishing a jig, a fish may be swimming toward you with the jig in its mouth, and it's time to set the hook.

Setting the Hook

The kind of hook you use makes a big difference in what you need to do when setting the hook. Different kinds of hooks allow you to do different things and are more effective in some kinds of situations than in others. Pick the right hook for the fish you want to catch.

ALERT!

Always be aware of the strength and condition of your line when setting the hook. Light lines require a lighter hook set than heavy lines. If there's any chance your line is frayed, a strong hook set will break it. Use enough force to drive the hook home without breaking your line.

Barbed Hooks

Hooks with barbs are made to hold the fish and not come out easily when you hook them. When fishing with barbed hooks you should set the hook with more force because you must drive the hook past the barb into the fish.

Barbs are in proportion to the size of the hooks, so a small hook will have a small barb and is easier to drive home. Big hooks for saltwater fish require a lot of force to make them penetrate past the barb. A stiff rod or a heavier line that doesn't stretch much helps drive the hook in. Use a hook appropriate for the fish, but stick with the smallest hook that will do the job.

Barbless Hooks

Hooks without barbs are required in many places, especially where catch and release is required. Many trout streams have barbless-hook regulations, so always check before fishing. Barbless hooks penetrate easily and come out of the fish's mouth easily without damage, but they're more likely to come out during the fight, too. With practice you can land fish just as well with a barbless hook.

Do I have to buy barbless hooks?
No. To make barbed hooks barbless, use a pair of pliers to mash the barb flat on the shank of the hook, or file off the barb.

QUESTION?

Double and Treble Hooks

Hooks on plugs are usually either double or treble hooks and are generally fairly small. Even so, these hooks can be hard to get into the fish's mouth and can also tear it. If you're losing a lot of fish when they jump, check the ones you do land to see if there is a big hole where the hook is in their mouth. If so, back off on your hook set a little. If there's not a big hole or if the plug comes out of their mouth easily after you land them because the barb didn't penetrate, set the hook harder.

Circle Hooks

Circle hooks are designed to hang in a fish's lip without requiring a hard hook set, minimizing the chance of hooking a fish in the throat or gut. First used on long lines in salt water where a line is baited up and left unattended, they hook fish well without jerking on the hook when you get a bite. Experiment with circle hooks and see if they work for you. They're very popular in salt water and many freshwater cat fishermen and bass fishermen use them, too, but some fishermen hate them. Some say they just don't work for them. Try them out and see if they fit your needs.

Importance of a Sharp Hook

The importance of a sharp hook can't be overemphasized. A sharp hook will penetrate the mouth of the fish better and enable it to go in past the barb. A sharp hook is not as likely to slide along the hard part of a fish's mouth and come out without sticking into it. And a sharp hook will sometimes stick and hold when a fish tries to spit it out.

Ways to Sharpen Hooks

Hooks can be sharpened to have a round point like a needle or a cutting point like a knife. There are pros and cons about each one, and some work better with different kinds of fish. Choose the best point for the way you are fishing but above all make sure the point is sharp.

A round point penetrates and slides into the mouth of the fish easily without making a big hole. Round points are best on soft-mouthed fish and are more common in freshwater fishing than in saltwater fishing. Most hooks come from the factory with a round point and can be very good, especially the ones that are super sharp. You still need to keep a check on them and sharpen them while fishing because many things will dull them.

FIGURE 14-1

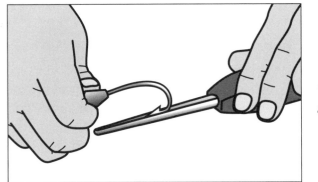

◀ Sharpening a hook.

Filing a triangular point on the hook makes a cutting point. The cutting edge should be toward the inside of the bend and the back or outside of the point should be flat. A hook sharpened like this cuts into the mouth of the fish when you set the hook and penetrates deeply. It can cut a hole that will allow the barb to come back out, though. Cutting points are best for fish with hard mouths and they are more common in saltwater fishing.

ALERT!

With either kind of point, don't sharpen it too thin on the tip. A very thin point will bend rather then penetrates if it hits some hard part of the fish's mouth. Keep the point sharp but not so thin it will bend.

To test for sharpness of either kind of point, drag it lightly across a fingernail. The hook point should catch on your smooth fingernail or scratch it, not slide along the nail. If it slides along your fingernail, it will likely slide along the hard parts of a fish's mouth. Don't put too much pressure on the hook while testing it. If it doesn't catch with very light pressure, it's not sharp enough, and you don't have to increase the pressure and risk cutting yourself.

Playing the Fish

Hooking the fish is just the first part of your efforts to land it. The way you fight the fish after hooking it is critical to getting it out of the water. Learn ways to improve how you fight fish and how to avoid basic mistakes, and you're more likely to land the fish that decides to eat your bait.

Ways to Lose Fish

After you hook the fish, many things can go wrong. What you do while fighting the fish after hooking it can determine whether you land it or get very disappointed. Some things that can go wrong after a fish is hooked include the following.

- The fish jumps and throws the hook.
- The hook pulls out of the fish's mouth.
- The fish gets caught in underwater obstacles.
- Malfunction in tackle causes you to lose the fish.
- The line breaks between you and the fish.

It's exciting to watch a fish jump, but don't get so caught up in the spectacle that you lose the fish. The fish makes the lure shake violently when it jumps, especially when caught on crank baits and top-water plugs that hang out of the fish's mouth during the fight. The shaking can make the hooks tear out from the weight of the lure. After setting the hook on a fish, keep your rod tip low. This lowers the angle of the line and makes it less likely the fish will jump. If you pull up on the fish while fighting it you make it more likely to jump. Go so far as to stick your rod tip under the water to keep the fish down.

An exception to this is when you're fighting big saltwater fish that jump a lot. You must "bow" to the fish when it jumps by lowering your rod tip and giving it slack. This helps to avoid breaking line if the fish falls on it. As the fish comes up out of the water you lower your rod tip, then pull back when it goes back down. Tarpon, marlin, and sailfish are good examples of fish that require a "bow."

There is often nothing you can do to keep a hook from pulling out during a fight. Sometimes the hook is in a soft part of the fish's mouth or the fish is not hooked well and the hook comes out. You can lessen the chance of that happening by not putting too much pressure on the fish. Don't pull hard against a running fish unless it's around cover and you must pull it away to avoid getting hung up. If that's a problem you'll have to put a lot of pressure on the fish to move it away from the obstacle.

Buying good equipment and keeping it maintained will help you avoid equipment failure that will lose fish. Make sure your reel is in good working order with no worn parts. Check your rod for nicks and cracks that will cause it to break when fighting a fish. Buy good hardware and make sure swivels, snaps, and split rings are a suitable size and not bent when you use them.

Your line won't fail you while fighting a fish unless you use line that's way too light for the fish you're catching. Line failure is usually due to abrasions on the line or a poor knot. Tie a good knot and check your line often to make sure it's not rough. Retie it regularly, too. When using very light line don't put much pressure on the fish and make sure your drag is set correctly.

Importance of Drag

The drag system on reels allows line to come off the spool while fighting a fish. This will prevent the line from breaking if the fish makes a strong run. The drag lets the spool turn and release line until the fish slows down, without giving the fish slack line that might help it get off the hook. To work well, a drag must allow line to come off the spool smoothly and consistently while the reel is in gear.

Spin-Casting Reels

Spin-casting reels usually have a poor drag system because their construction makes it difficult to design a drag system that works well. The spool must turn inside the reel to allow line to come out, and the angle the line makes going around the edge of the spool and out the hole in the cover fights against a smooth drag. The drag usually consists of a small tab that works against notches in the side of the reel. The spool moves in jerks between notches and is not consistent.

Spinning Reels

Spinning reels come with either front or rear drag systems that are made up of alternating metal and fiber or plastic washers that work against each other. Front-drag reels have bigger washers and are smoother but are harder to adjust during the fight. Rear-drag reels are easy to adjust but have smaller washers, meaning they are not as smooth. You need to adjust the drag when fighting a strong fish because as line comes off the spool the drag gets tighter as the amount of line on the spool gets smaller.

FACT

Back reeling is a way of allowing fish to take line from a spinning reel that gives you control over the way it goes out. As the fish pulls you let the handle turn backwards and play out line. You can control the amount of line that goes out with the reel handle and immediately start reeling again when appropriate by turning off the antireverse.

Bait-Casting Reels

Bait-casting reels usually have a star drag that is controlled by a star-shaped fitting under the handle. It's made up of different kinds of washers inside the reel that rub against each other as the spool turns while the reel is in gear. They can be very large and the drag system on bait-casting reels is usually smooth and consistent.

You can also control the drag on a bait-casting reel by using your thumb against the spool and putting the reel into free spool. Pressure of your thumb on the spool acts as the drag and controls the amount of pull that's needed to take line. This can be a dangerous way to fight a big fish because you must take the reel out of gear during the fight to do it. Ⓔ

Chapter 15

E Landing and Handling Your Fish

Y ou've caught the fish—now what do you do? Do you plan on releasing the fish? If so you don't want to injure it. Are there parts of the fish that will hurt you? If so you don't want to injure yourself. Choose the best way to land the fish based on what you plan to do with it.

Protecting the Fish

The methods of landing a fish described in this chapter offer you various options for getting the fish to you without hurting it *or* you when you land it. It's important to play the fish correctly and land it unharmed if you plan on releasing it. A long battle builds up toxins in a fish's body so you should get it to you as quickly as possible.

Fish have a protective coating of slime on them that keeps them from getting infections on their bodies. You should land the fish in a way that wipes as little of this slime off its body as possible. You should never lay it down on the ground or in a boat because the contact will damage the slime layer. Also be careful how you hold the fish. Any place you touch the fish with your hand will remove some of the slime. The position you hold the fish can injure it, too, especially if you're posing for pictures. And the longer you keep it out of water the more likely it is to be injured, so you should get it back in the water as soon as possible.

FACT

Holding a bass by its lower jaw and twisting it so it's parallel to the ground is a common way to pose, but this can break the jaw or stretch the muscles of the fish's mouth so badly it won't be able to feed. You should never twist a fish, especially a big one, by its jaws.

When releasing the fish, ease it into the water and move it back and forth to run water across its gills until it's able to swim off. Don't throw the fish back into the water and make it hit hard on its side, because that can injure it, too. When fishing high above the water on a bridge or pier it's almost impossible to release a fish without injuring it.

Protecting Your Hands

Many fish have sharp fins, teeth, and gill plates that will hurt you if you're not careful. The gill plates on some fish can be as sharp as a razor and cut you badly. Even the skin on some fish can scrape and cut you. If you are not familiar with the type fish you're catching be extremely careful with the way you handle it. Landing the fish is a dangerous time because you're usually excited, trying to get it out of the water quickly, and you can do things that expose your hands and the rest of your body to the dangerous parts of the fish. You can use any of the landing devices we'll talk about shortly to help protect your hands while landing a fish. But once the fish is out of water, you still have to touch it regardless of what landing device you use. Bottom line: Always be careful when touching a live fish.

ALERT!

Bass fishermen often grab a bass by its lower lip to land and hold it. Don't do this with a fish you aren't familiar with until you look in its mouth, especially if you're in salt water. Some freshwater fish and many saltwater species have teeth that will cause serious injury.

Landing by Hand

Landing a fish by hand is quick and works well with some kinds of fish. But it can be dangerous to you if the fish has parts of its body that can hurt you. Learn which fish can be safely landed by hand and then decide if it's appropriate for the way you're fishing.

Good Points about Landing by Hand

Landing a fish by hand is the quickest way to get it out of the water, and you have more control over it than when it's flopping around in a net or on a gaff. Some species of fish, like bass, bream, walleye, pike, and flounder, lend themselves to landing by hand. Bass have a nice big lip to grab; small bream can be grabbed by their bodies and bigger ones by the mouth; walleye and pike have teeth, but you can put a finger in their gills to pick them up and hold them; and flounder can be pinched on either side of the gills (but don't stick your finger in their mouths).

Releasing a fish after landing it by hand is quick and easy, and requires a minimum of handling. Since the fish is already in your hand, you can put it back in the water and revive it easily by moving it back and forth.

Bad Points about Landing by Hand

Some fish are impossible to land by hand. Big saltwater fish like swordfish and sharks can't be landed by hand because they're too big to handle. It's common in salt water to release many kinds of fish like tarpon without ever actually landing them because of the danger to you and the fish. They're considered caught when the fisherman or the mate on the boat touches the leader.

Big-game fish that are brought into the boat too soon or that jump while being landed can severely injure and even kill anglers. Learn how to handle big-game fish from experts and let the crew handle them if you go out on a charter.

It's easy to injure a fish by holding it wrong. Not only can you break its jaw, you can damage gills and eyes by pinching the fish there. What's more, when a struggling fish moves in your hand as you try to land it, you can easily clamp down too hard on it and damage it that way.

Bending over to hand-land a fish is very awkward on the shore and on a boat. You can lose your balance and possibly hurt your back; or the fish can move wrong and jam a hook into you. Many anglers have hooks stuck into their hands, arms, and legs while landing fish.

Using Nets

Using a net is one of the most common ways to land fish in fresh water, but is not as common in salt water. Nets come in many sizes and shapes for different kinds of fishing and most fishing boats will have one in it. Most nets are made of nylon cord netting. Some have handles and some hang on ropes, but all are made to hold the fish while taking it out of the water. There are also special kinds of nets made of rubber to reduce the chance of injuring the fish.

FIGURE 15-1

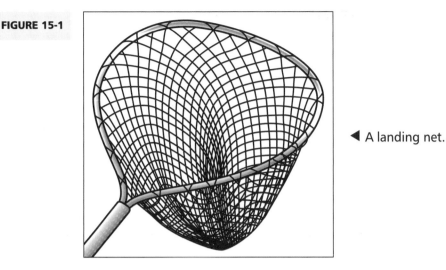

◀ A landing net.

Good Things about Nets

Using a landing net makes it much easier to land a fish. The fish is securely held in place while you bring it in, and you can scoop up the fish without having to touch it. Nets even make hook removal easier because the fish is not able to move around as much in the net.

If you're fishing with another person, that person can get the net while you fight the fish and be ready to net it as soon as you get it in. There's less chance the fish will shake off the hook right at the boat because you can net the fish underwater. And you can land the fish faster with a net than you can with your hand, and avoid wearing it out as much, which is better for the fish.

FACT

As a fish fights, lactic acid builds up in its body. The longer it fights the more the acid builds up. If too much of it is produced, the fish will not be able to survive when it's released; so shorter fights are better for the fish.

A fish can't back up very fast so you should always net it headfirst. The person fighting the fish can lead it into the net if the netter holds the net underwater. Trying to scoop up a fish in a net, especially if chasing it from behind, is a good way to lose it.

When using a circular net from a bridge or pier, you should have it just under the surface of the water. Lead the fish over the net headfirst, then raise the net quickly. You can then pull the fish up without taking a chance it will break your line or come unhooked as you lift it. It's much easier to land a fish this way if you have someone helping you do it.

Bad Things about Nets

Hooks tangle in nets and can be difficult to remove. A fish that twists and turns as it fights can tangle the hook as it wraps the net around its body, making it difficult to remove both the fish and the hook. That means more chance of getting a hook in your hand as you unwrap the fish and try to untangle the hook.

ESSENTIAL

Plugs with treble hooks are especially apt to tangle in the net. To avoid tangles, if the fish is small enough, you can raise the fish with the line while holding the net under it. For bigger fish, a good option is a special rubber net made to help prevent the hooks from tangling.

Nets remove the protective slime from a fish while landing it, especially when the fish struggles. Nylon nets are worse at damaging the slime on fish than are rubber nets, which are more popular for catch and release. But in general, if you plan on releasing the fish, you probably shouldn't use a net to land it for its own safety.

When fighting a strong or big fish it's easy to lose it while trying to net it. Some ways you can lose a fish at the net include:

- A fish can swim under the net and fray your line on the net.
- The hook can get tangled on the outside of the net and the fish can pull off.
- A fish can see the net and make a strong run and break your line.
- You can touch the fish with the net and make it run hard and pull off.

- A fish can tear an old net and go through it.
- A fish can jump over the net and throw your hook.

If a partner is trying to net the fish for you and one of these things happens, it's real easy to blame your partner. But losing a fish at the net happens and there's nothing you or your partner can do about it sometimes.

Be Careful with Gaffs

Gaffs are made to stick into the fish and hold it so you can land it. Gaffs are big hooks on the end of a handle and allow you to reach down and grab the fish. Some are made to stick into the mouth of the fish and others are made to hook into its body. On some gaffs the hook remains on the handle as you bring the fish in; on flying gaffs, the hook attaches to a cord on the handle, and the cord comes off when the fish is gaffed, so you land the fish by pulling in the cord.

FIGURE 15-2

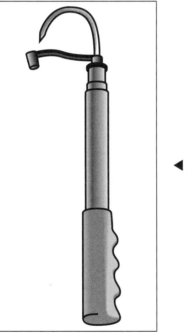

 ◀ A gaff.

Good Things about Gaffs

A gaff is a good way to secure a big fish and get it into the boat. The handle of a gaff will support the weight of a large fish, and a flying gaff with the hook attached to a rope can be used to land very large fish. When fishing from a big boat with high sides, using a gaff allows you to reach down and get a solid hold on a fish and control it. Gaffs are also good for use from docks and piers if they're not too high above the water.

FACT

The point of a gaff must be kept sharp and a cutting edge is best. When trying to penetrate the side of a big fish like a king mackerel, the point must be sharp enough to go through the scales and any bones it hits to go deep enough to securely hold the fish.

Bad Things about Gaffs

Gaffs stick into the fish and injure it. Even if you lip-gaff a fish, there's damage done to it and it's less likely to survive. Gaffs are sometimes hard to stick into the fish and must be kept extremely sharp, especially the ones made to hook into the body of the fish. And gaffs can break or pull loose, causing you to lose a fish that is mortally injured.

Gaffs are usually used in saltwater and the blood released in the gaffing process can attract sharks. The sharks may get your next fish before you have time to land it. Having a shark eat the fish you're trying to land is not something you want to happen, but it's a fact of life for saltwater anglers.

Lip Grips: a Practical Alternative

Lip grips are a relatively new landing device. There are several different kinds available but all have a set of jaws that penetrate the soft tissue of the fish's mouth and clamp shut, allowing you to land the fish without touching it with your hand. Some have built-in scales so you can land the fish, weigh it, and release it immediately.

Good Things about Lip Grips

A lip grip holds the fish and allows you to lift it from the water without touching it, meaning you won't damage the slime layer. The fish hangs from the lip grip in a natural position that does not injure it and it can swing freely so there should not be any damage to the jaw or muscles of the fish's mouth.

Transferring a fish from a net to a scale puts more stress on the fish. A lip grip with a built-in scale eliminates this problem and weighs the fish more accurately than gaffs and nets with similar built-in scales. It's a very simple process to land, weigh, and release a fish with a lip grip.

A lip grip is easier to handle when fishing by yourself since it's compact and operated by only one hand. And the fish is much more secured and your hand is safer than when you hand-land a fish.

Bad Things about Lip Grips

The fact that a lip grip must penetrate the flesh of a fish's mouth means some damage is done to the fish. Although putting a hole in the soft tissue of the mouth of most kinds of fish will not do permanent damage, it can allow infections to start. And if the fish is very big its weight can tear the hole even bigger during landing.

ALERT!

Lip grips are banned in some tournaments. If you're fishing a tournament, be sure to check the rules before using a lip grip to land fish for you or your partner.

You need a strong grip to clamp the jaws shut on models that require you to squeeze the handle shut, and you also need a strong grip on models that open when you squeeze the handle and the jaws close on release of the handle. When using a lip grip, all the weight of the fish is in one hand, so you need to be strong to handle a big fish. And lip grips rely on some kind of mechanical action so failure is possible, meaning you can lose a fish if yours fails.

Landing with a Cradle

A cradle is a special kind of device for landing long fish that you don't want to injure. It's most popular for holding a muskie beside the boat while you take the hook out of its mouth. The cradle looks like a small stretcher with netting or canvas between two long poles. It's put into the water beside the boat and the muskie is lead over it. When the two sides are brought together they cradle and hold the fish securely. A cradle is almost impossible to use if you're fishing alone, though. Another person is needed to put the cradle into the water and hold it while you fight the fish and bring it to the boat.

Wear Gloves

Wearing gloves can protect your hands and allow you to land a fish without danger to yourself. Some gloves with special gripping surfaces are made especially for landing fish. There are even gloves that will stop the sharp teeth of fish from penetrating to your skin. Work gloves are good for grabbing huge catfish by the mouth.

Good Things about Gloves

Gloves are cheaper then most other fish-landing devices. You can purchase work gloves for just a few dollars, and they don't take up much space, either. You can purchase several pairs of gloves and keep them with your tackle.

Wearing gloves and landing fish is as close to hand-landing as you can get and still protect your hands. You retain most of the positive things about hand-landing without exposing your hands to injury. And they keep your hands clean, avoiding the slime that makes it necessary for you to wash your hands before starting to fish again.

Big saltwater fish are often released by pulling them alongside the boat with the leader and then removing the hook without ever bringing them into the boat. Gloves allow you to hold the leader without hurting yourself and also help in removing the hook without exposing your bare hands to teeth or rough skin on the fish.

Bad Things about Gloves

Gloves remove slime from fish much worse than bare hands do, which exposes the fish to greater infection. And you lose some feel through gloves, meaning you may squeeze harder than necessary to hold the fish, which will likely injure it even more.

Gloves are awkward to put on while fighting a fish. If fishing alone you would have a hard time holding the rod and controlling the fish while trying to put on a glove to land it. Wearing a glove can make handling the rod and reel very hard to do, meaning you're more likely to lose the fish before landing it.

Holding a Fish

Holding a fish presents many of the same problems as landing a fish by hand. You don't want to injure yourself or the fish while holding it. There are ways to remove hooks without creating problems or exposing yourself to dangerous fins and teeth. And there are ways to pose for pictures to enhance the shot without harming you or the fish.

Always look where you're putting your fingers. Holding a bass with your fingers works fine but fish with teeth can't be held that way. Putting your hand in the gills of a pike works but if your fingers go too far inside they can damage the fish, and the gill rakers will cut you.

Hook Removal

Removing hooks creates special problems in handling fish. You need to hold them securely and take the hook out of their mouths. If you're keeping the fish, it doesn't matter if you squeeze them tightly with a glove and jerk the hook out with a pair of pliers; but don't do that if you plan on releasing the fish, because you'll seriously injure them.

Needlenose pliers are a staple in every fisherman's tackle, and they're useful for removing hooks as well as doing other jobs. But for removing hooks, a hook disgorger is a better tool. This is a device with a squeeze handle that operates little jaws at the end of a long shaft. You can dislodge the hook by grabbing it with the small jaws and twisting it out from the mouths of fish with teeth without getting your hand too close. A jaw spreader, a simple wire spring that holds the fish's mouth open, will help, too.

Posing for Pictures

When posing for pictures with your catch, hold the fish carefully, avoiding parts that might hurt your hand. Hold the fish up just below your chin in front of you or at eye level beside you, and let the fish hang naturally if you're holding it with one hand. Don't try to twist is sideways unless you put your other hand under the body to support it. If you plan on releasing the fish, remember that each place you touch the fish is another place you damage the slime layer and expose the fish to infections. Hold the fish toward the camera some because that makes it look bigger. Always get the eye of the fish in the shot, because the picture won't look right without it.

Don't keep the fish out of water any longer than absolutely necessary if you're going to release it. The longer it's out of water, the less likely it is to survive. Dip the fish back under the water if there's a pause between shots. Keep it wet and keep the gills in the water as much as possible.

If you plan on keeping the fish to eat, it will taste better if you put it on ice immediately. Keeping the fish in the water on a stringer or in a live well is not as good as cooling it off quickly. Handle a fish you plan to eat as little as possible, not to protect it, but to protect its flavor. Ⓔ

Chapter 16

Cleaning and Cooking Your Catch

If you release your catch, your fishing trip is over when you go home. But if you keep some fish to eat, there are a few things left for you to do. Cleaning, cooking, and eating your catch are the next steps and some of them are more pleasurable than others.

Cleaning Fish

A traditional way to clean a fish it so scale it and gut it. This method produces a whole fish and the head can be cut off or left on. Small fish such as bream in fresh water and croaker in salt water lend themselves to scaling, while bigger fish can be cleaned in other ways. Some recipes are done better with whole fish.

How to Scale and Gut a Fish

Keeping fish wet until it's time to scale them helps make removing the scales easier. Make sure the fish stay wet by putting them in a live well, which is an aerated container filled with water for transporting fish, or on a stringer in the water. A stringer is a cord with a pointed metal shaft on one end to slip through the gills of the fish. There is usually a metal ring on the other end to keep them from sliding off, but you should loop the line back through the ring on the first fish to attach it securely. Even better, put the fish on ice as soon as you catch them to keep them moist and help preserve their flavor.

To scale a fish, lay it on its side and rub the edge of a dull knife or spoon against the grain of the scales, working from tail to head. You can hold the fish by the head or purchase a clip board to hold it. Wearing a glove on your holding hand will keep the fish from slipping. The scales should peel off easily as you scrape against them. Work carefully around the fins so you do not stick a fin in your hand.

FACT

Some fish, such as trout and flounder, have tiny scales that are very difficult to remove and are okay to eat as is. The skin can be removed after cooking or skin and scales can be eaten without a problem.

To gut bigger fish, make a cut with a sharp knife from the vent opening to the head, and then scrape the guts out with a finger or a dull knife. Many people like to cut out the vent hole itself during this process for esthetic reasons; cut a V-shaped notch across the body of the fish to cut it out. If you're going to cut the head of the fish off, do that first and then make the cut up the belly of the fish. Cut from the top of the head around the back of the gill plate to the neck of the fish just below the eye in a semicircle, cutting all the way through the fish.

On small panfish like bream, crappie, and croaker, it's much more efficient to make a diagonal cut from the top of the head to just behind the vent across the fish and all the way through it. This removes the head and guts with one stroke of the knife, and it's very easy to remove any remaining guts in the body cavity. Cutting a fish in this manner loses very little meat.

After the Cleaning Is Done

Check all around the fish for remaining scales and scrape them off; then wash the fish with cold water to remove any loose scales and guts. Cook the fish immediately for the best flavor or put it in salt water in the refrigerator if you are going to cook it within a couple of days. Make sure the entire fish stays in the salt water so it doesn't dry out before you cook it.

You can freeze small fish whole, submerged in unsalted water if you want to keep them for several weeks. Cut the top out of a milk jug and put the fish in it; then cover it with water and freeze it. Don't use plastic bags because the fins will stick holes in the bag and make it leak.

Filleting Fish

Filleting a fish produces a bone- and skin-free piece of meat that's easy to cook and store. Most fish can be filleted easily, from small panfish like perch to huge saltwater fish like grouper.

Fish taste different in different waters and sometimes a bad flavor from their environment, and even pollutants, can concentrate in the skin. It's often best to remove skin and bones from fish when cleaning them, and filleting is a good way to do this.

How to Fillet a Fish

To fillet a fish you need a sharp thin-bladed knife and a flat work surface. You can buy a good fillet knife, keep if very sharp, and use it for nothing but filleting fish. The point as well as the blade should be sharp. A board two feet long and twelve inches wide works well and you can wash it easily after use.

FACT

Many people use an electric knife for filleting fish. The electric knife works well, stays very sharp, and since the blades are removable it cleans up very easily. You don't need a sharp point on an electric knife because the blade slices right through scales and bones.

FIGURES
16-1–16-4

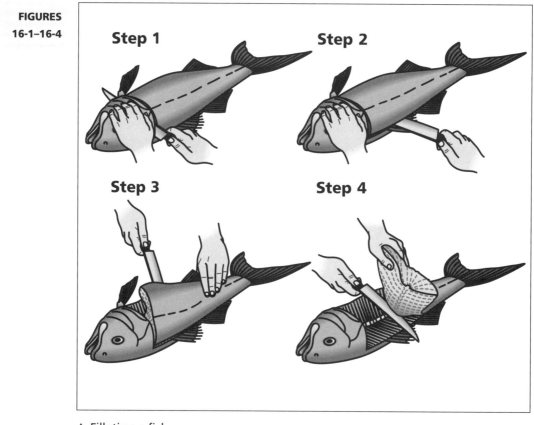

▲ Filleting a fish

Step one: Lay the fish on the board and make a cut just behind the gills across the body down to the backbone. On a small fish this cut will cross the whole body; on a bigger fish you will need to move your knife to make a complete cut. Be careful you don't cut through the backbone, especially when using an electric knife.

Step two: With smaller fish you can turn the blade of the knife and follow the backbone all the way to the tail, skipping steps two and three. With bigger fish make a cut along the top of the backbone with your knife, following it all the way to the tail. This cut will guide your knife and make it easier to cut the fillet off the fish.

Step three: Make a similar cut along the belly of the fish, staying above the anal fin. Keep your knife parallel to the board and run the point of the knife right along the bottom of the backbone. Continue this cut past the ribs.

Step four: Make a cut from the head of the fish all the way to the tail, cutting through the ribs where they attach to the backbone. For a skinless fillet you should stop just before cutting through the skin at the tail. Flip the fillet over and, holding the tail, run the knife between the skin and meat starting at the tail; then remove the skin. Turn the fish over and repeat the process on the other side.

For a boneless fillet, cut out the rib cage by running the point of your knife along the top of the ribs at an angle, cutting them away from the meat of the fillet. There's very little meat on the ribs of smaller fish.

After the Filleting Is Done

Boneless, skinless fillets are easy to cook or freeze. You can cook them immediately for the best flavor or refrigerate them for a couple of days in a plastic zipper bag filled with salt water. Put the fillets in the bag, add a tablespoon of salt, some water, and then squeeze the air out as you close the bag. Be sure to rinse the salt water off them before cooking.

You can use the same process for freezing but don't add the salt. They will keep for a year, but the longer you keep fish the less flavor they have, so use frozen fish quickly.

Skinning and Steaking Fish

Catfish and other smooth-skinned fish have to be skinned before you cook them. You can buy special pliers that pinch the skin and give you a good grip on it. Cut through the skin all the way around the head of the fish just behind the gills and pull the skin toward the tail. If it tears just grab it again at the tear and start pulling.

ALERT!

When cleaning catfish, be extremely careful of their spines, which can make deep puncture wounds that get infected easily. It's a good idea to clip the top fin and the sharp ends of the side fins before starting to skin catfish.

Hold the fish by the mouth with a glove or by placing your fingers under the side fins of a small catfish. An even better method, especially on a big catfish, is to nail its head to a tree or skinning board to hold it while you pull off the skin. Nailing the head to a stable surface allows you to grip the skinning pliers with both hands while you skin a big, tough fish.

Steaking is a good way to clean big fish like salmon or halibut. Scale or skin the fish first and then cut steaks across the body, or pull the skin off each piece after steaking the fish. Start just behind the gills and cut all the way through the meat and backbone. Continue down the fish cutting the steaks into the thickness desired and stop before the pieces get too small. You can then fillet out the tail or cook it whole.

After you clean the fish, you've got the waste parts to dispose of. Many people who clean their fish on site throw the guts back into the water, but make sure this is legal.

Frying Fish

Frying fish is a traditional way to cook them and big fish fries are common in many areas. Fish can be pan-fried or cooked in deep fat. There are even special fish cookers designed to fry a lot of fish at one time. Many restaurants feature fried fish but you can fry them yourself at home, and they're even better.

Frying—Good and Bad

Fried fish taste excellent and are a favorite of many people. At home it's easy to fry fish because all the equipment and ingredients are handy. On the down side, you often don't have either available to you away from home. Fried fish smells up the house, the added grease isn't good for you, and all that grease is usually a cleanup problem.

Ways to Fry Fish

Small panfish can be fried whole in a pan or deep fryer. Bigger fish should be filleted or steaked to make frying easier. Rinse off the fish or fillet, dry it on paper towels, and then roll it in cornmeal. It's even easier to put the cornmeal in a sack, drop the fish into it, shake it up, and take out a piece of fish well-coated with the meal.

Use one part flour and three parts cornmeal; add pepper and salt to taste. Include a little paprika or chili power for a different flavor if you like it. You can add other things to the coating mix, or you can purchase ready-made coating mixes at the grocery store. You can also mix up a batter of egg, milk, and flour, dip the fillet in it, and fry up a moist fillet similar to what you get in fast-food restaurants.

Make sure the grease in the deep fryer or the pan is very hot, almost to the smoking point at about 370 degrees Fahrenheit. In a deep-fat fryer just drop the fish in and watch it turn brown. For pan-frying lay the fish in a pan of hot grease that covers it halfway. Turn it over when one side is brown.

FACT

You should fry fish about five minutes per inch of thickness, so a two-inch-thick fish should be taken out of a deep fryer after five minutes or turned over after five minutes in a pan. Don't overcook fish because it gets dry and tasteless.

Baking and Broiling Fish

Whole fish, fillets, and fish steaks all can be baked or broiled in an oven. Baking fish in a covered pan keeps moisture and flavor in. Broiling fish gives them a nice brown top but also keeps them moist. Many different seasonings can be added to fish when cooking in the oven to add different flavors to it.

Baking and Broiling—Good and Bad

Fish has been proved to be a healthy food, and baking and broiling are both healthy ways to cook them. Many people like the way fish tastes baked and broiled with nothing added. Or if you like, you can add just a little spice to improve the taste without adding calories or fat. Baking fish is easy: Cover the fish to retain moisture and flavor, and you don't have to keep a close watch on them. Broiling browns fish fillets and makes them a little drier, which is preferred by many people.

On the downside, baked and broiled fish usually have a stronger fish flavor than fish cooked other ways, and some people find it objectionable. Oily fish are often too strong to taste very good when baked or broiled unless something is added to them to cover the taste. Broiled fish can burn quickly and must be watched carefully

Ways to Bake and Broil Fish

Fish with mild white flaky meat like crappie, flounder, bass, and grouper are very good baked or broiled. For stronger-flavored fish, more seasoning needs to be added. For mild fish a few drops of lemon juice and maybe a pat of butter is all many people add. A little paprika or chili powder sprinkled on the fish before broiling or baking makes for an interesting flavor.

For an oven-fried taste, try rolling a fillet in some kind of stuffing mix and then baking it. This gives the fish a very good flavor and spices it up some. You can also stuff a whole fish with dressing or lay it on a bed of dressing to bake. Covering a fillet with salsa, picante sauce, or some other kind of tomato sauce can be an interesting way to cook it.

For oily fish like bluefish and striped bass, cover the fillets with bacon strips and onion rings before baking. The bacon and onion remove the strong fish flavor and give it a good taste. Also try other strong-tasting spices on strong-flavored fish to cover the fishy taste.

Grilling Fish

A salmon steak cooked on a charcoal grill is hard to beat, and grilled fish are a staple of many waterside restaurants. Grilling fish gives it a special flavor and is a good way to cook many kinds of fish. Fire up the grill, add a few fish steaks, and eat as if you're at a restaurant on the beach.

Grilling—Good and Bad

Cooking fish outdoors keeps the house cool in hot weather and keeps odors outside. Grilling gives fish a very good flavor all its own. Cleanup is easy and cooking is simple.

On the downside, charcoal used for grilling can add chemicals to the meat, and fish tends to tear apart when you turn it on the grill. It's more difficult to adjust the temperature of the grill and harder to get the fish done without overcooking it. And finally, weather can be a factor in your comfort while cooking outside.

Ways to Grill Fish

The simplest way to grill fish is to lay a steak on the grate of the grill and let it cook. You can rub it with oil or spices before cooking to give it extra flavor and keep it moist. Basting during cooking with butter or oil will also keep it moist. Marinating fish before cooking it will change and enhance the flavor of some fish. Brown one side and then turn it to brown the other side. Try not to overcook the fish.

FACT

A special kind of holder is made for grilling fish. It consists of two long handles with a flat grill at the end of each one. You place your fish on one of the grills, close the other grill on top, hook them together, and you can turn the fish over without tearing it up when one side is done.

You can also wrap the fish in foil and cook it on the grill. The foil seals in the moisture, which is similar to baking inside in the oven. Add onions, tomatoes, butter, peppers, and other ingredients to change the basic flavor. This also eliminates the problem of turning fish on the grill when one side is done, and cleanup is very easy.

Soups and Stews

From light bouillabaisse to hearty chowders, there's a fish soup or stew to fill any appetite. Almost any kind of fish can be used in soup or stew, and you can add many kinds of ingredients to go from an appetizer to a full meal. Most areas of the United States and countries of the world have their own special kinds of fish soup and stew so you can get a flavor of other places by exploring recipes.

Soups and Stews—Good and Bad

How you make fish soup and stew is limited only by your taste. Cooking fish in stews and soups is a good way to make use of smaller parts of fish that might otherwise be wasted. Frozen fish work well in soups and stews so you can use those that have been frozen for a while rather than cooking them some other way. Soups and stews even freeze well for later use.

The only bad thing about stews and soups is they just don't last long enough. Some people don't like the taste but you can find recipes that lower the fishy taste, so there should be some kind everyone would enjoy. If someone says fish stew tastes bad, try a different recipe.

Ways to Make Fish Soups and Stews

Traditional soups and stews are either milk or tomato based, with fish and seasonings but little else. Stews can include everything from potatoes to peppers, and can be as mild as you want or hot enough to please anyone's craving for fiery food.

Boil some fillets, shred the meat, and simmer them in milk or tomato soup for a simple fish-based soup. Cut the fillets into chunks and add boiled potato cubes to the milk based-soup for a New England–type fish stew. Use mild white fish for a less fishy taste.

For a hearty Manhattan-style stew, cook potatoes, tomatoes, and corn in fish stock and then add chunks of fish during the last few minutes of cooking. Make a gumbo by adding okra to the mix. Put in some chili powder or hot sauce to spice it up. Use a little fish or a lot, depending on your taste.

Boiled fish can be excellent. Boil a mild white fish such as bass until it's done; then dip pieces in butter or cocktail sauce as an appetizer. Some say it tastes like boiled shrimp, but it has a good flavor even if you don't think it tastes like shrimp.

Pickled and Salted Fish

Pickling and salting of fish have been around for a very long time. Pickled fish is preserved in a vinegar solution, and salted fish is persevered in layers of salt. For centuries salting was the only way to preserve fish for shipment or to carry with you on journeys. Pickled and salted fish have a flavor all their own, and you can use both of them at home.

Pickled and Salted Fish—Good and Bad

To preserve fish without refrigeration you can pickle or salt them. This is a cheap way to keep them, and they will last a long time. Salt fish can be cooked in many recipes and pickled fish are a good appetizer.

On the downside, the salt added to fish is hard to remove and is a health problem for some people. Some pickled fish has a very strong fishy taste that some people dislike. Pickling takes a long time to be effective so you can't eat the fish immediately; you must wait several days. And salt fish can turn rancid, which ruins its flavor.

Ways to Pickle and Salt Fish

You can make your own salt fish by layering fish and salt in a glass or wooden crock. Do not use metal because it will react with the salt. Don't use table salt with iodine added. Layering the fish and covering them with salt pulls the moisture out of the fish, and it will keep for a long time. When you want to use the fish, soak it in fresh water to remove the salt, changing the water several times before cooking the fish.

Ceviche is a pickled fish that many people enjoy. Fillets are put into a wooden or glass bowl and lime juice or vinegar, onions, and bell peppers are added. After the fish turns white from the pickling process it's eaten as an appetizer. You can also place small fish like bream in jars with vinegar and other spices to pickle them, and some people like the flavor.

Smoked Fish

Smoked fish is a delicacy you can make at home. Using a commercial smoker or homemade one, fish can be smoked and eaten immediately or smoked long enough to preserve them. Many kinds of marinades are used for flavoring the fish, and different kinds of wood are burned to produce various smoky flavors. Fish can be smoked whole or cut into fillets or steaks for smoking. Carp are very good smoked, and you can get the small bones out of carp more easily after smoking. All kinds of fish can be smoked but oily fish seem to do better. If you don't want to make your own, you can buy smoked salmon in many stores. Use smoked fish in dips or eat it as a main course. Ⓔ

Chapter 17

E

Angling Laws and Etiquette

There are laws that govern how many fish you can catch, how big they have to be, and what equipment you can use. There are even seasons controlling when you can fish for certain species. Beyond the laws are traditions and customs having to do with the consideration fishermen normally give one another.

Fishing Seasons

Seasons are usually set to protect fish during the spawn. During closed seasons it's illegal to fish for specific species, and those caught accidentally while fishing for other kinds of fish must be released immediately. Seasons vary widely in different areas and for different kinds of fish.

When freshwater fish spawn they're often very easy to catch because they move into shallow water and many try to eat anything that comes near their nest. If enough spawning fish are caught, they might not produce enough young to replenish the population. Even if the fish are released after they're caught they might not spawn successfully.

If there are huge numbers of fish in a body of water there may be no closed seasons because enough young are produced no matter how many adults are caught. For example, in the South, fishing for bream while they're spawning is a common activity. Although prohibited in many northern states, fishing for bass on the spawning beds is also allowed in the South where growth rates and survival rates are higher.

Seasons on saltwater fish are also set to protect them during the times when they are spawning. Many kinds of saltwater fish have no closed season but some of the more desirable fish do. These seasons are in place to allow them to spawn and produce future catches.

Endangered species may not have any open season at all, so they are protected year round.

FACT

Fish are usually divided into two groups: game fish and nongame fish. Nongame fish may include fish that are caught commercially and fish that are undesirable for eating or for sport. Limits are different for different kinds of fish.

Creel Limits

The word "creel" refers to the wicker basket used to carry fish, and "creel limits" is a general term referring to the number of fish you're permitted catch. Laws govern the numbers of fish you can keep each day as well as the total number you can have in your possession for the entire fishing trip. These laws are based on the numbers of fish in certain bodies of waters and how fast they can reproduce and rebuild populations. Limits are set to ensure the fish have a sustainable population for future fishing.

Daily Limits

Daily limits control the number of fish you can catch and keep in one day. The numbers vary widely depending on how prolific the fish are in a particular body of water. Some species like crappie and whiting have very high limits; others like bass and redfish are much more restricted. The biologists at the Department of Natural Resources set these numbers, usually with some input from fishermen.

Creel limits are on a per-person basis, and each person fishing can keep that number. Some people get around the limits by taking young kids and other nonfishing family members with them and catching the limit for each person; but ethical fishermen and game wardens frown on getting around the law this way.

Some species of fish may be so plentiful that there is no limit on them. If an undesirable or non-native species of fish gets started in a body of water, to encourage elimination of the species, often no limits are set on them to encourage fishermen to keep all they catch. If a species of fish has a high limit, that tells you they should be easy to catch and you shouldn't worry about keeping as many as you want.

Possession Limits

Laws governing fishing also control the number of fish you can have in your possession. Sometimes the possession and daily limits are the same but often the possession limit allows you to have more fish. This allows fishermen making weekend trips to keep a limit each day, up to a certain total for the whole trip. The limit is usually low enough, often two or three times the daily limit, so that fishermen can't keep huge numbers of fish and claim they've been fishing for a long time.

Possession limits also allow fishermen to take advantage of seasonal fishing patterns where one kind of fish may bite good for a few days then disappear for the rest of the year. The authorities try to strike a reasonable balance between allowing a fisherman to keep fish to eat and not harming the fish populations. Most fishermen don't try to keep large numbers of fish, and sport fishermen usually don't keep enough fish to be concerned with possession limits.

Size Limits

Size limits are placed on different kinds of fish for different reasons. Some size limits are set to allow fish to grow old enough to reproduce. Others are in place to allow the harvest of smaller fish but protect bigger fish that spawn. And some special limits are set to encourage fishermen to remove fish of a certain size to improve the population dynamics of a body of water.

Minimum Size Limits

A minimum size limit is the most common one in most areas. Bass have minimum size limits in most states and some states have a lake-by-lake size limit on bass, usually somewhere between twelve and sixteen inches. Some saltwater fish also have minimum size limits that can be surprising to freshwater fishermen, ranging from twelve inches for fish like Spanish mackerel and bluefish to almost five feet for fish like tarpon.

FACT

Bass tournaments usually have a minimum size limit of twelve inches unless the local limit is higher. This is to ensure fishermen bring in bigger fish, and to protect the resource. Most bass tournaments also have a five-fish creel limit, usually lower than the local creel limits, for the same reasons.

Minimum size limits make you release fish shorter than that limit. This ensures a good population of fish below a certain size for slow-growing or hard-fished species. The minimum size is often just above the size where that species starts spawning. Some fisheries have a minimum size set on certain species to allow fish to grow to trophy size. Those waters usually have a very low creel limit, allowing only one fish, if any at all, to be kept.

Maximum Size Limits

Some species of fish don't reproduce until they get very big, so a maximum size limit is often set for them. This allows larger fish a better chance to survive and spawn, ensuring more fish for the future. Redfish often have a maximum size as well as a minimum size, ensuring some fish reach a quality size before being harvested and also protecting the bigger spawning-age fish. Striped bass are another species that often has a maximum size limit.

Slot Limits

Bodies of water sometimes have unbalanced populations of fish where it's beneficial to try to increase the numbers of fish in a certain size range. To do this, slot limits are set, allowing anglers to keep fish under and above a set size, but requiring the release of all fish in the slot size. This can stockpile fish of a specific age and size range while reducing fish that are smaller.

ALERT!

On lakes with slot limits, too many fishermen do not keep smaller fish below the slot size, but keep only the larger fish over the slot size. This defeats the purpose of the slot limit and hurts the lake in the long run. Keep the smaller fish as the fisheries biologists recommend.

Bass are one of the most managed fish in fresh water and they often have slot limits placed on them. A lake that has a slot limit of eleven to fourteen inches would mean you could keep bass shorter than eleven inches and longer than fourteen, but those in the slot must be released. On lakes with high reproduction rates but slow growth rates for bass, this would allow thinning the numbers of small fish while protecting a group of a size that could take advantage of bigger prey fish.

Catch and Release

There are several good reasons to mandate catch and release. Some species of fish are valued as game fish but aren't good to eat, so it's good for sport fishermen to have some waters where they can catch trophy fish but not keep them. And some species of fish grow slowly enough and are fished hard enough that it is necessary to protect all adults. Also, many fishermen believe it's better to enjoy catching fish and then release them to fight again.

Catch-and-Release Laws

Big-game fish in the ocean are often governed by mandatory catch-and-release laws. These fish are rare enough and less desirable to eat, so catch and release makes sense. In the past, fishermen were allowed to keep one trophy fish to mount; but now that fiberglass reproductions are available, there's no real reason to keep the trophy fish. Marlin, sailfish, and tarpon are good examples of fish that are often mandated catch and release.

Some trout streams are trophy waters where you must release every fish you catch. This ensures that big fish are put back into the water to be caught again. Some bass waters are also catch and release for the same reason. This concept will work on smaller bodies of water but probably can't be effective in bigger lakes and salt water since fish can move to different waters where protection isn't guaranteed.

Catch and release of game fish that grow slowly and have a low reproduction rate also works to allow some fishing for them but protects them, too. Although low creel limits can help, not allowing any fish to be kept is more efficient for some fish. Although some kinds of big-game fish are good to eat, using them for food is not an efficient use of the resource, so catch and release is mandated.

Voluntary Catch and Release

Bass fishermen have long practiced catch and release, and tournaments have encouraged it to the point at which it's a sacrilege to keep a bass in many places. This actually works to harm fish populations in some smaller bodies of water. If bass overpopulate, they can't get enough food, so they won't be healthy and generally won't grow very fast. In larger bodies of water, however, catch and release probably makes no difference to the fish populations.

To be worthwhile, catch and release must be tailored to the specific bodies of water and populations of fish in those waters. Releasing fish after a tournament was started as a publicity tool to combat the image of professional fishermen killing large numbers of fish, and to avoid giving animal rights groups something to use against fishing. For tournaments, it's a good idea to continue to release all fish to avoid any accusations; but the individual fisherman who keeps a few to eat shouldn't be ostracized unless the person keeping the fish is doing so illegally.

In salt water, catch and release has long been a way of life for big-game fishermen, even before it was required. It makes little sense to bring in a tarpon to the dock and kill it just to show it off. Tarpon are not very good to eat so there is no need to keep them. But you can keep many excellent-tasting fish, such as croaker, which also have high creel limits.

Fishing Licenses

Fishing licenses, which are issued by the state, are usually required of fishermen over sixteen years old, and many states give licenses free to senior fishermen. Some states require licenses to fish in salt water while others don't. Most states charge nonresidents higher fees for fishing licenses than they do residents. Be sure to check local requirements before going fishing.

Special license requirements are often in effect for different species of fish. Trout fishing usually requires a trout stamp in addition to the regular license. Many states also have public fishing areas that require additional license fees and permits to fish. Generally the more management required of a species of fish the more likely additional stamps will be required to help pay for the additional cost.

Many states have specified "free fishing days" each year when you can go fishing without a license. These are set up to allow people to try fishing and to encourage more people to take up the sport. Watch your local paper and check state regulation books for free fishing days in your area.

In most states money collected for fishing licenses goes to the state Department of Natural Resources for managing and improving fishing. Fees are usually reasonable and are used to make sure you have more fishing opportunities, so you shouldn't mind buying the required licenses.

Illegal Equipment

Equipment that is not sporting and takes large numbers of fish is not legal to use. Laws governing such equipment vary from state to state and are tailored to the needs of different locations. Most illegal methods are not something sport fishermen would want to do anyway, but some people want to find ways to take fish to eat without the challenge of catching them.

Telephoning—Another Name for Shocking Fish

Telephoning fish got its name from old hand-cranked telephones. When a person cranked the handle it produced an electric current, and fisherman found that they could drop the wires into the water and shock the fish. The fish would float to the top to be scooped up. Theoretically, the fisherman could go to a hole in a creek or river and shock up every fish in it.

There's nothing sporting about catching fish in this manner. You simply scoop them out of the water. And you can take all the fish in an area. This method of taking fish has been outlawed since it was first found, but some people still use it today.

FACT

Game and fish biologists use shocking as a legitimate way to count fish. They use a generator rather than an old telephone and send electric current through two booms out in front of a boat. Every fish between the chains hanging down from the booms come to the surface to be counted. They can be released after the count since the current does not kill them.

Traps Can Be Illegal

Fish traps are allowed in some locations for some kinds of fish but other places outlaw them completely. Traps are more common in salt water and can catch large numbers of fish at one time. Saltwater traps are often very big and consist of weirs. Freshwater traps are usually smaller basket-shaped devices for catching minnows and catfish.

Baskets can be used to catch catfish but the legal design makes it less likely game fish will go into them. Simple baskets with an open funnel at one end are usually outlawed, and baskets with trap doors and double funnels are required. In salt water, traps are used to catch many kinds of nonfish species like crabs and lobster, but they can be used for fish, too.

Minnow traps used to catch bait are usually legal but must comply with strict laws. You're regulated on the size, shape, and number of traps you can put out for bait. And you're required to check them regularly so the minnows in them don't die. A trap can be a fun and efficient way to get bait, but you're required to release any game fish you catch.

Certain Nets Are Illegal

Seines and gill nets are often illegal in fresh water but are allowed more often in salt water. The length and mesh size of nets are usually regulated if the nets are allowed at all. Gill nets work to tangle fish when they try to swim through the mesh, so requiring the mesh to be a certain size ensures fish larger and smaller than the mesh are not caught. Game fish can usually escape from a short seine so seine length is regulated to control what can be caught in it.

Cast nets are often used to catch baitfish and are about the only way to collect them. These nets are shaped like a parachute with weights around the edge. When thrown over a school of fish they sink fast and a rope pulls the bottom together around the fish. Any game fish caught in them must be released immediately. In some areas, especially salt water, you're allowed to take some kinds of game fish like mullet with a cast net.

Illegal Hooks

Some states make double and treble hooks illegal and also regulate the number of hooks that can be attached to one line. Some trout streams have single-hook regulations to protect the fish, especially in catch-and-release streams. The hook usually has to be barbless in these streams, too. There are few restrictions on hooks in salt water.

Using hooks to snag fish is illegal in most fishing. Fish running up rivers to spawn are easy to snag under bridges. Fish on the spawning bed can be snagged. And big schools of saltwater fish are often thick enough that snagging works on them, too.

A big treble hook with a lead weight on its shank is usually used for snagging. It's lowered into the water and jerked up sharply, hooking into any fish that's swimming over it. It injures the fish and catches any size and species that happens to be there. Some states and provinces outlaw the selling of big treble hooks for this reason.

Snagging is legal for a few kinds of fish, like paddlefish, because certain fish can't be caught any other way. Some states have very strict laws that allow snagging certain fish, and only those fish, during a limited time each year.

Sharing Information

Fish tales are common and stories about the one that got away or the numbers of fish caught are heard every day. It's almost required that you exaggerate some when talking about fishing, so you should take everything you hear with a grain of salt. But if you want to receive valid information in return, you should be careful to stick with the truth.

While You're Fishing

Some things are shared by fishermen while they're fishing, but other things are kept secret. It's fine to ask what fish are biting and how deep, and you'll usually get accurate responses. But if you ask the exact location fish are biting, you'll probably get a strange look and bad information in return. Fishermen generally don't want to share their secret fishing holes with anyone.

Sharing information about where fish are feeding is more common in salt water than fresh water. You can often get on a marine radio and find out where others are catching fish, and fishermen in salt water are more likely to give you exact locations where they caught fish. It is not unusual to share GPS (Global Positioning System) readings and chart coordinates among saltwater fishermen.

Dock talk is famous in bass tournament circles. Many tournament fishermen will intentionally mislead other competitors by making up things, changing the truth just enough to throw others off, and bragging to intimidate them. If you listen to too much talk at the dock you may be mislead, especially if there's a tournament going on.

Talking one-on-one is a better way to get valid information. Try to get to know fellow fishermen and don't be too pushy when talking with them. Also talk with dock and bait store owners, but be willing to share your information with them if you expect them to share with you.

Over the Internet

Telephoning friends to tell them what you caught and how has been a way to share information for a long time. Many people call fellow fishermen before going fishing to find out what they should do. Recently, computers have taken over for sharing information, and chat rooms and bulletin boards give you access to a wide range of fishermen. You can often get invaluable information this way.

ALERT!

When going to chat rooms and bulletin boards to get information, take some time to learn the rules and accepted practices there. If you go in and violate rules and customs you're unlikely to be welcome or to get accurate information.

The same things apply to sharing information at home as on the water. Be honest with people you want accurate information from in return. Try to get to know them before asking too many questions. And be willing to share what you know with them.

Chapter 18

Boats and Motors

A boat and motor will give you access to many places to fish in both salt water and fresh water that you couldn't get to without them. Boats and motors are expensive and range from tiny one-man crafts to huge oceangoing big-game trollers. Pick a boat and motor that fits your fishing needs and it will give you many happy hours of fishing.

What Kind of Boat

Choosing the right kind of boat for your fishing can be tough, especially if you do a lot of different kinds. If you fish both salt water and fresh water it's almost impossible to find a boat that will be suitable for both. If you compromise and get a boat that's good for a lot of different kinds of fishing you may not be happy with it for any of them.

Freshwater Boats

You must match the size of your boat with the size of the water you fish, for both safety and convenience. Since freshwater fishing ranges from tiny creeks and ponds to the Great Lakes, no one boat will be suitable for every water you might want to fish. You'd be surprised how many fishermen have at least two boats. A big bass boat will allow you to fish bigger bodies of water like rivers and lakes, and can even be used in the bays of the Great Lakes if you watch the weather. They're good for bass, crappie, walleye, pike, muskie, and other kinds of fishing. Because they're not suitable for ponds, small creeks, and shallow rivers, many bass boat owners also own a small jon boat (a small flat-bottomed boat) for fishing small waters.

If you live near a big body of water like one of the Great Lakes you need a boat suitable for fishing open water. Boats for the Great Lakes often are the same as saltwater boats and are similar in size since the same kinds of conditions are met on them. If you fish open water regularly, buying a big boat will be a good choice. If you go out only a few times a year it would be better to go on commercial boats or find other people with boats and offer to share expenses.

FACT

When trying to choose a boat, think about what you'll use it for most. It's often better to get a boat designed for most of your fishing and adapt it to fishing you do occasionally, rather than get a boat that is a compromise of several types of fishing and does nothing well.

Kinds of Freshwater Boats

Boats have been designed for many different kinds of fishing. Some are used for specific applications and aren't much good for anything else; others are very adaptable and can be used in a wide variety of types of fishing. Here are some kinds of boats used for fresh water, along with their good and bad points:

- **Bass boats:** Small one-man bass boats less than ten feet long are good for small waters, and they're stable but are hard to carry very far. Bigger two-man bass boats must be trailered to fishing holes, but they're stable and take rough water fairly well. They're very comfortable to fish from and are easy to maneuver with an electric motor. They'll also get you where you're going in a hurry, but aren't suitable for the conditions you sometimes encounter in the Great Lakes.
- **Canoes:** Canoes are good for getting into tight places and can be used for fishing in smaller rivers with rocks. They can be carried to waters inaccessible by road. But they're not very stable so it's very difficult to stand and fish from them.
- **Jon boats:** Jon boats are stable and work well in smaller bodies of water that don't get very rough, because they don't handle big waves very well. They can be carried, but not as easily as a canoe.
- **Open-water cruisers:** Big open-water cruisers are suitable for big lakes like the Great Lakes but are expensive to buy and maintain. Many are big enough to sleep on and can be used for more than fishing.
- **River drift boats:** River drift boats are big and heavy and must be carried in by vehicle, but they handle big rivers well. They're also very stable fishing platforms.
- **V-hull fishing boats:** V-hull fishing boats take waves better than flat-bottomed boats like bass and jon boats, but aren't as stable. They're good for fishing in waves and work well in rivers.

Saltwater Boats

Small freshwater boats can be used for inshore fishing where bays and rivers are protected from the ocean, but they can be dangerous.

Bigger boats are usually needed for saltwater fishing and some have been developed for specific applications. Center-console boats are made for standing and steering and many are big enough to go well offshore.

If you want a boat to use mostly in salt water, make sure all fittings are stainless steel and it's designed for saltwater use. Salt water is tough on boats and you need one that has been designed to withstand the corrosive effects of it.

Cuddy-cabin boats give you the added benefit of a protected area to get out of the weather. Many in the twenty-five- to thirty-five-foot range are used for fishing near the coast, especially in the Gulf of Mexico. For offshore fishing on the Atlantic or Pacific you'll need a large boat designed for handling high seas and rough weather. These are a major investment and few novice fishermen start with them.

Saltwater boats are big enough that they usually are stored near the water, either in docks or boat houses on land. It's expensive to keep them even if you don't use them because docking and storing fees are not cheap. Unless you plan on doing a lot of saltwater fishing it is better to go on charters and party boats. You can go once a month on a party boat (a boat that takes out fishing parties) for less than the monthly storage fee in most cases.

Safety Around Boats and Motors

Safety should be the first consideration when using boats and motors. There are several pieces of equipment that you should have mounted on your boat and motor or carry with you at all times. Some are required by law and others are required by good sense. They can save your life.

Staying Safe on Boats

Every boat is required by law to have a life jacket for each person onboard. These life jackets should always be kept within easy reach.

There's often no time to open a locker and take out life jackets in emergencies. Keep them near the people who may need them and make sure each person knows how to get into them quickly.

ALERT!

Children should always wear a life jacket while on boats and around water. Even if they're beginning to learn to swim and you watch them carefully, make them wear the life jacket at all times. Don't take a chance with their lives.

Fire extinguishers are also required on most boats. Be sure you know how to use one and that it's in good working order. You should be able to quickly put out any fire that starts on a boat before it endangers you, so keep the fire extinguisher where you can reach it quickly if you need it.

Some kind of sounding device is also required on most boats. Bigger boats have built-in horns, and you can carry small compressed air horns or whistles on smaller boats. Sounding devices are used to warn other boats away if they're approaching too closely and also to signal for help if you're in trouble. Radios and cell phones can also be used to call for help, but they are not required on boats.

Safe Handling of Motors

Motors can have two devices that help you control the boat. Kill switches hook to the key or electric system of the motor and kill the motor if you pull a cord. If you have the kill switch attached to you and are thrown away from the steering wheel or tiller, the motor will stop. This is extremely important if you're thrown out of the boat because the boat will start running in circles and come back and run over you.

A foot throttle allows you to control the speed of the boat just like in a car and means you can keep both hands on the steering wheel rather than driving with one hand and having the other on the hand throttle. Most bass boats are equipped with them and any fast boat would be safer with a foot throttle. Keeping both hands on the steering wheel is safer than using one hand.

Boat Accessories

Boat accessories can range from instruments to show how the motor is operating to fancy outriggers to aid in fishing. Some are necessary for almost all boats while others have specific applications. It's best to start small and add accessories when you decide you need them.

Accessories for Safety and Comfort

A small jon boat with an electric motor does not need many accessories, whereas an offshore trolling boat will need a lot. With bigger motors you need a gas gauge, tachometer, speedometer, and water pressure gauge. A motor with a tilt and trim unit will need a gauge to show its position.

Ropes and anchors are necessary in all boats to tie up at docks or to hold you in position in open water. If your motor fails, anchors can act as safety devices to keep your boat facing into the waves and also to keep you from drifting too far. Paddles are nice to have even on big boats because they can be used to push off from docks and banks as well as paddling in the water. A boat hook can be used in the same way and also help you dock bigger boats.

Comfortable seats can make the difference between a fun, relaxing fishing trip and one that wears you out. Most bass boats have elevated seats on casting decks where you can sit and fish in comfort. Fighting chairs on big-game saltwater boats are a necessity to be able to stand the long fights with big fish. And an ice chest can be used for food and drink as well as storing fish you want to keep.

Fishing Accessories

Downriggers and outriggers are good accessories for many conditions. Downriggers allow you to get a bait down to deep fish and keep it there while trolling. Outriggers spread baits in a wide pattern and allow you to use more rods while trolling. Nets and gaffs are needed to land many fish.

Live wells are very useful for keeping your catch alive until it's time to ice it down; they're required on all bass boats used in tournaments. Bait tanks are great to use if you do a lot of live-bait fishing. Rod holders around the gunnels of the boat will allow you to troll or still-fish several rods at one time without taking a chance on losing them.

A temperature gauge will help you determine how active fish should be and also find water temperatures that are better to fish. Some devices such as pH meters, color meters, and light meters have been popular in the past but are not used much any more. Rod lockers and tackle storage bins help keep the boat organized and safeguard equipment.

Fishing Made Easier with Electronics

A few years ago fishermen went out and tried to catch fish without the aid of many of the electronics available today. For many modern fishermen, casting without a depth finder in easy sight is like casting blindfolded. You can check the depth of the water, see structure that holds fish, and even see the fish themselves with a good depth finder. With other modern equipment, you can find specific locations and even mark a spot electronically and return to it.

Depth Finders

Depth finders show you the bottom and everything in between by using sonar technology. Displays range from a flashing light spinning around a dial to liquid crystal displays and paper charts. Some depth finders are weak and show only depth, others are so strong you can watch a quarter-ounce jig going up and down at thirty feet under the boat.

Transducers are the antennae of the depth finder that send out and receive the signal. They show what is directly under them. Place the transducer near the back of the boat for the view there or place it on your trolling motor to see what's directly under where you're standing.

A flasher is the most basic kind of depth finder. A light spinning around a dial lights up each time an echo is returned from an object below, and you can learn to interpret these flashes. They will show you fish, objects on the bottom, and even how hard the bottom is. It does take some study to learn how to read a flasher.

A paper graph depth finder has a metal stylus that moves across a paper chart as the paper moves. It leaves a mark on the paper each time an echo is received, giving you a permanent record of what's under the boat. Graphs are usually more powerful with stronger signals than flashers and easier to read since you can study the paper.

The most popular depth finders today are liquid crystal display units. A screen shows a picture much like the paper graph; the screen changes or scrolls just like the paper graph but isn't stored. These depth finders can be set to show small fish pictures when they receive echoes from an object not connected to the bottom. This can be misleading since many things other than fish might send back such an echo.

Depth finders are a must on almost any kind of fishing boat if you plan on fishing anything but visible cover. They show you hidden spots that fish like, and good ones will actually show you the fish. You can also find schools of baitfish. Learn to use one to improve your fishing. They work well in both fresh water and salt water.

Location Devices

For years a compass was about the only tool fishermen used to find their way from one place to another. Line-of-sight triangulation was used to mark fishing spots. In open water, finding a brush pile or reef that you had fished before required a lot of luck.

In recent years several devices have become available to give fishermen amazing tools for navigation and locating spots. Loran was one of the early ones, but Global Positioning System (GPS) has become the way to navigate. This system uses satellites to locate your exact spot with a receiver. It's so accurate you can mark a brush pile in the middle of a lake, then go back to it later and arrive within a few feet of it.

Hand-held GPS units are so accurate they contain maps that show you where you are and where you're going. You can put in courses as you go, and return along the exact same course. These units show speed and will even estimate your time of arrival when navigating to a point.

You can get hand-held units for about $200 and units that mount to the boat and work with your depth finder for $500 to $1,000.

Many lake and marine maps have GPS coordinates on them to help you locate fishing spots. Drop-offs, underwater humps, and rocks are marked in fresh water and reefs, wrecks, and other fish-attracting spots are marked in salt water. You can add your own spots to the ones given on the maps and charts. Ⓔ

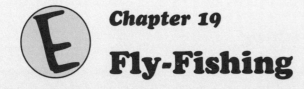

Chapter 19

Fly-Fishing

Fly-fishing is almost a different sport from other kinds of fishing. The equipment and baits are very specialized and generally not interchangeable with those used for other kinds of fishing. Although any kind of fish can be caught on fly-fishing equipment, some species are more traditional than others. Fly-fishermen seem to have a different attitude toward fishing, too.

Why Is Fly-Fishing Different?

Fly-fishing developed as a sport rather than a way to put food on the table. It's a much more visual sport than most other kinds of fishing and often more like hunting than fishing. Fly-fishermen often stalk an individual fish they see feeding and try to outsmart it with a fly that imitates its food. And fly-fishermen first developed the concept of catch and release.

The Sport of Fly-Fishing

There's a difference when you go fishing if the goal is to catch something to eat rather than just to have fun catching fish. Fly-fishing seems to be more about fishing for sport than catching fish for food, and most fish caught are released to be caught again. Fly-fishermen have reverence for the fish they catch, treating them gently and trying not to harm them.

The challenge in fly-fishing is to get the fish to accept an artificial bait, often one you made yourself, as food. Once that challenge is met the fight of the fish becomes important. Rather than pulling the fish in and landing it quickly and efficiently, the fly-fisherman gets the most fight possible.

FACT

Tying their own flies is an important part of the sport to most fly-fishermen. Many study the craft of tying flies and the habits of insects as much as they study the habits of fish. They can identify almost any kind of insect a fish will feed on and match it to the appropriate fish.

The Attitude of Fly-Fishing

Fly-fishing is more of a solitary pursuit than are other kinds of fishing. Although several friends may go fishing together, for most freshwater fishing, they split up and fish alone. It's difficult for more than one person to fly-fish from a boat at one time, so one person fishes while the other maneuvers the boat. Even in saltwater fishing where a boat is necessary there is usually a guide that controls the boat while one person fishes.

Fly-fishing seems to be a more contemplative sport, too. The classic image of a fly-fisherman is someone standing in a pristine trout stream all alone, with nothing but the sounds of nature. The fly-fisherman concentrates on fishing and the actions trying to get the fish to hit, and nothing else. The simple fly-fishing equipment doesn't create much of a disturbance and the fisherman becomes one with nature.

For many years fly-fishing was considered an expensive sport only for the few to enjoy. But today's modern equipment is inexpensive enough for anyone to fly-fish, and TV shows and books have taken some of the mystery out of it. As more and more people learned to fly-fish, it has become less intimidating, so more fishermen are willing to give it a try.

Learning to Fly-Fish

There are many ways to become a fly-fisherman, from reading a book about fly-fishing to going to an expensive school. Teaching yourself from books and videotapes works, but having others share their knowledge is a better way to learn. If you're lucky enough to have a friend willing to teach you, you can learn from your friend's experience and avoid mistakes. Going to a school is the next best thing to having a friend teach you.

Learning from a Mentor

The traditional way to learn fly-fishing is for a family member or friend to teach you. If you're lucky enough to know such a person, that person can teach you the basics and take you to some of his or her favorite waters. Sharing fishing knowledge is a common way the sport is perpetuated.

ALERT!

Learning from a friend or family member is a good introduction to fly-fishing but be careful you don't pick up any bad habits or limit yourself to what your mentor knows. Always be open-minded; add to your skills by reading about and studying other ways to fly-fish.

If you know someone who fly-fishes, you may be able to meet others who are willing to share their expertise with you. Fishing clubs are a good way to meet other fly-fishermen to share knowledge with. Hanging around fishing stores that specialize in fly-fishing is another good way to meet people who might be willing to share. Don't be too pushy, respect others' desires, and you might find a mentor who will train you in many things about fly-fishing.

When you are starting out fly-fishing don't hesitate to ask for guidance and information from fellow fishermen on the water. Don't interrupt their fishing but approach them while they're taking a break or after the fishing day is over. Try to be friendly and let them know you're willing to learn. Most fishermen like to share their favorite sport with new people.

Fly-Fishing Schools

There are many fly-fishing schools available to you and they can be great ways to learn the sport. From local clubs and sporting goods stores that often hold classes lasting a few hours, to water-training vacations that teach you for several days, you can find one that's right for your budget and time available. You'll be exposed to the knowledge of more than one expert, which ensures you will get a broad selection of ideas and methods.

Consider recruiting a small group to go to a school together to learn. That way you can share information among yourselves and you may be able to get a group rate. Sharing a room with a friend and working with an instructor together can be a cost-effective way to learn.

Many resorts have classes and take guests to local fishing spots. Try to schedule your family vacation at a place that offers classes in fly-fishing as well as other activities all family members will enjoy. You can also hire fly-fishing guides who will teach you on the water.

Specialized Equipment

The equipment used for fly-fishing is very specialized and it takes some practice to learn to use it correctly. It's more important to match rod, reel, and line when fly-fishing than in any other kind of fishing. The reel and rod must be balanced in weight and the line must be the correct weight for the rod you are using. Rods are marked with the line weight they cast best. And fly-fishing is different because you cast the line, not the lure. The line must be heavy enough to cast, and you have to use a leader with it to separate the thick fly line from the lure.

Long, Limber Rods

Long, limber rods are needed to fly-fish and they come in different weights that you use for different kinds of fishing. A two-weight fly rod is considered ultralight and is used for casting very small flies, for catching smaller fish. An eight-weight rod is very heavy and is used for casting large flies, for big fish. Saltwater rods are even heavier and made for bigger fish and bigger baits.

Generally the lighter rods are shorter and don't cast as well into the wind. They're best for smaller waters and making shorter casts. Heavier rods are better for open waters and work better when there is some wind that you must cast against. The longer the rod, the longer the cast is a good general rule of thumb.

Fly rods come in many price ranges, too. Graphite rods generally cost more than fiberglass rods, and handmade bamboo rods are too expensive to use for anyone but the purists with lots of money. To start fly-fishing in fresh water for most species of fish, choose an inexpensive rod in six-weight that is about eight feet long. It's a good rod to learn on and will handle most kinds of fish without costing too much.

FACT

Check at local and mail-order sporting goods stores for inexpensive starter fly rod outfits. You can usually get a cheap rod, reel, and line for under $100 to get started. If you like fly-fishing and do enough of it to justify the cost, you can get a quality outfit for the kind of fishing you do.

A Choice of Reels

Reels are single action, multiplying, or automatic. On single-action reels, the spool turns one time each time you turn the handle, retrieving a short amount of line. On multiplying reels, a gear system turns the spool faster than the handle is turned, bringing in line faster. Automatic reels are spring-loaded and bring in the line when you press a lever.

For most fly-fishing the fly reel is there to hold the line and nothing else. You pull line off the reel by hand then cast it using the rod and you fight fish by stripping in line by hand. The line is reeled back on the spool after the fight is over. When fighting strong fish that make long runs, you'll need a fly reel that has a drag system, and you'll use it to fight the fish. Steelhead in fresh water and many kinds of fish in salt water require fly reels with a good drag system.

Saltwater reels must be made of noncorrosive materials and also must be strong enough to stand the high pressures of fighting a powerful fish. You'll need a large-capacity reel that holds many yards of backing as well as the fly line. Freshwater fish usually don't pull all the fly line out unless they're extremely big. Many kinds of saltwater fish will strip all your line off to the backing.

It's important to match the size of the reel to the rod and to the fish you're after. The reel should balance the rod so the rod doesn't tip toward either end when it's balanced on a finger held just above the reel where your casting hand will be. A balanced rod and reel will keep you from getting as tired while casting. The reel must be big enough to handle all the line you will need, as well as the pressure from the fish you're fighting, but not so big as to make the outfit too heavy at the reel end of the rod.

Lines Are Important

Fly line is important because it's what you cast, it controls whether the fly floats or sinks, and it controls how deep or shallow your bait goes down. Different kinds of lines allow you to make long casts with heavy wind-resistant flies, or to delicately place a tiny gnat on the surface of the water. Some fly lines are good for many kinds of casting while others are very specialized.

Fly lines come in weights just like rods. A one-weight fly line is the lightest and most delicate, while a fifteen-weight is mostly for saltwater big-game fish. For most of your fishing, a line in the midrange should be suitable, so look for something from four- to six-weight. Lines at that weight will handle everything from trout flies to bass bugs, and once you decide on the kind of fishing you will do, you can go to lighter or heavier line that will be better for specific types of casting.

Line and rod weights should match for best performance. You can go a little one way or the other when matching them up, but don't stray far apart in numbers. Keeping them together will give you the best results.

There are special fly lines for special jobs, too. Floating lines float and are used for flies that float, like bugs and dry flies, or flies that are fished near the surface like nymphs and streamers. For fishing deeper you need a sinking line, which come in different sink rates. Sinking lines are much harder to use than floating lines so stick with floating lines when you start fly-fishing.

ESSENTIAL

Shooting-head lines are special lines that are heavier toward the end. They're useful for making long casts, which is what the name comes from. The heavy end on the line makes it shoot forward on the cast, resulting in longer casts. Weight-forward lines are similar but have less weight on the end so you can make a more delicate presentation even though you can't cast quite as far.

Monofilament Leaders

Leaders used to connect the fly to the fly line are made of monofilament line. They're thin and clear and less likely to spook the fish than the thick heavy fly line on the rest of the reel. Leaders can be a few feet long for fish that are not easily spooked, or many feet long for line-shy fish. For finicky trout, a two-pound test leader might be required, while a thirty-pound leader would be too light for some salt-water fish.

Tapered leaders are thicker at the line end and thinner at the fly end to make the fly act properly at the end of the cast. You can buy tapered leaders or tie your own. Bought leaders are quick and easy to use, but tying your own gives you flexibility to adapt to changing conditions.

Light Lures

Flies are usually small, light lures made of hair or feathers. They're wrapped and tied to a hook in such a way that they resemble something a fish feeds on. A dry fly floats and looks like an insect sitting on top of the water. Nymphs sink and look like the nymph version of an insect underwater. Streamers sink and are made to resemble small bait fish.

Fly-fishermen go to great length to match the fly to what the fish are feeding on, especially when trout fishing. Trout can be very finicky eaters and won't hit something that doesn't match what they're eating at the time. At other times they'll hit streamers and nymphs, which you can use if you can't determine exactly what the fish are feeding on at the time.

Saltwater fishermen usually use streamers because they resemble the baitfish the fish feed on. Saltwater streamers can be huge when fishing for big saltwater fish, often bigger than the trout sought by other fly-fishermen. White is a very common color for saltwater streamers because most saltwater baitfish have some white or silver in them.

With all flies, from those tied on a tiny #22 hook for small stream trout to a bucktail tied on a 6/0 hook for marlin, the hook must be very sharp. Using relatively light rods and line requires a sharp hook to penetrate the mouth of the fish with little pressure. Keeping a sharp point on your hook can often mean the difference between a strike and a hook-up.

Kinds of Fish

Almost any kind of fish that swims in fresh or salt water can be caught on a fly rod. They range from tiny trout in fresh water to tremendous tarpon in salt water. Fly-fishermen can learn what fish eat and tie a fly to match almost anything. If a fish is a good fighter fly-fishermen will figure out a way to catch it.

Freshwater Fish

Trout are the most common fish caught by fly-fishermen and they are the traditional quarry. From rainbows that are stocked in streams to cutthroat in the high Rocky Mountains, trout are a preferred game fish. It takes a lot of skill to catch trout, especially if they're fished a lot, so fly-fishermen work hard to catch them in many cases. Steelhead are rainbow trout that have gone out into salt water or the Great Lakes to grow and then return to rivers and creeks to spawn. They are a favorite of fly-fishermen.

Warm-water species like bass and bluegill easily fall to popping bugs and other flies and fly-fishermen catch large numbers of them. It's even possible to catch carp on fly rods by matching an insect they're feeding on. When the cicadas hatch, carp go on a feeding spree and fly-fishermen can catch them easier than at any other time.

Salmon are another traditional quarry of fly-fishermen and many streams where they run are limited to fly-fishing only. Some species don't feed while in rivers and streams so special flies designed to attract them are needed. They can be caught on flies even though they don't eat while spawning.

Fish that normally stay deep are harder for fly-fishermen to catch. Hybrids and landlocked striped bass can be caught by trolling with a fly rod but are more exciting to fish for when they are schooling on top. They will readily take a streamer when chasing baitfish. Walleye can be caught at times by casting minnow imitations to them when they're shallow. Even catfish can be caught on fly rods, but anglers usually have to resort to live or prepared bait to catch them.

Fish in Salt Water

Saltwater fish that can be caught on fly-fishing equipment are even more varied than freshwater fish. Big-game fish like marlin and sailfish are caught using fly equipment as are sea bass and cod. Even flounder fall to fly-fishermen. Fishing the flats in Florida has long been a favorite of fly-fishermen. Bonefish make sizzling runs that test the drag of any fly reel and tarpon, with their spectacular jumps and bulldog runs; these fish test the skill of the fishermen and their equipment. Specialized equipment is needed, but fighting fish like those offers a thrill of a lifetime.

FACT

The International Game Fish Association record book lists more than 105 species of saltwater fish and more than 90 species of freshwater fish in their fly rod section. Each species has several tippet, or leader test, classes, too.

Most kinds of saltwater fish feed on smaller fish so streamers that imitate them are the most common kind of fly used in salt water. You have to vary only the size to catch everything from swordfish to sharks. It's harder to get close to saltwater fish so you need shooting-head lines and long rods, but the thrill of hooking huge saltwater fish and landing them on a fly rod is worth it.

Types of Waters to Fly-Fish

Although most fishermen think of trout freshwater streams and saltwater flats as fly-fishing waters, fly-fishermen catch fish from anywhere fish swim. Small swamp ponds ringed by cypress trees filled with moss have fish that will fall to a fly, and so does the open ocean where the only thing you can see is wave after wave. You should be able to find suitable fly-fishing waters near you.

Tiny trout streams holding nothing bigger than nine-inch trout have a group of fishermen dedicated to fishing them. Almost any river or stream will have fly-fishing opportunities, and you can wade and fish many of them. Lakes and ponds are full of fish that will hit flies but boats are helpful to get to them. Try fly-fishing anywhere you find fresh water.

In salt water your options are more limited since you have to get to the fish with a boat in most cases. Although you can wade flats and fish with a fly rod, a boat is needed to get there and it's often easier to fish from one. Inlets and bays may offer some wade-fishing but a boat is helpful there, too. And big boats are required for big-game fish in open water.

Using Waders

Waders deserve a special note because they're needed in many kinds of fly-fishing, and can be dangerous. Water is often cold where fly-fishermen fish, so to protect their legs they need something that will keep them dry and warm. Hip boots and chest waders will do that, but you must be careful when wearing them

The bottom of rivers and streams is usually slippery and dangerous. Rocks are especially likely to make you slide down. Wear appropriate footwear and be extremely careful when wading in any kind of water, no matter what you're wearing.

Hip Boots

Hip boots are tall rubber boots that come up to you thigh or higher. They're good for wading in water that's no deeper than the hip boots are tall. There's some kind of strap or buckle to hold them on your leg and the foot end usually has a boot on it. Some come in stocking feet and you can wear wading shoes with them.

Most useful in shallow waters, hip boots allow you to fish streams that are not very deep, or have enough shallow areas that you can fish. Wear wool pants and socks under hip boots to protect you from the cold water. Hip boots are easier than chest waders to put on and take off and to get out of in a hurry if you get into trouble.

Special floatation devices are made specifically for wading fishermen. They attach to your belt and don't get in the way but will inflate if you go under. Always wear some kind of floatation device when wading. It can save your life.

Chest Waders

Chest waders come up to your chest and are held on by suspenders over your shoulders. They allow you to fish much deeper water and stay dry but can be very dangerous. With either hip boots or chest waders, stepping into a hole that is deeper than the waders are tall will fill them with water.

Chest waders come with boots attached or as stocking feet so you can wear wading boots or shoes over them. They are loose enough to wear warm wool pants and socks under too help keep you warm in cold water. Chest waders are also used when fishing from a float tube to keep you dry.

Chapter 20

When to Go Fishing

The best time to go fishing is whenever you can. Beyond that rule of thumb, some seasons and times of year are best for fishing for different kinds of fish. Freshwater fish respond to changing weather and feed better at different times, and saltwater fish move in seasonal migrations that bring them near you at different times.

Fishing with a Group

Joining a group that sponsors regularly scheduled fishing trips is a good way to go on a regular basis. There are bass clubs in almost every area, and they usually schedule monthly tournaments. Walleye clubs also have regular tournaments. Saltwater clubs usually schedule several trips a year. There are even sportsman clubs that schedule outings for different kinds of fish depending on what's biting.

Not only will joining a club give you a schedule to stick with, you'll have a chance to meet other fishermen and learn from more experienced ones. It will also give you access to a boat in many cases and even private fishing spots. To find a group to join, check with local sporting goods stores and watch your local paper for reports about club and group activities.

Spring Fishing Is the Best

In spring many a young person's fancy turns to fishing. Spring is often the best time of year to go fishing because many species are very active when the water first starts warming up. Fishermen are ready to get out and take advantage of the better weather after being cooped up by winter weather, too. You're ready and so are the fish, so spring is one of the best seasons to fish.

Freshwater Fishing in Spring

Many species of freshwater fish respond to warming water in the spring to find places to spawn, and they start feeding more actively. Ice-out (the time when water is first free of ice) is a well-known time of heightened activity for many species of fish in the North, and you should take advantage of it if possible. Most fish start feeding heavily as soon as the water starts to warm no matter where they are. Water warming from the fifties may indicate spring in the South whereas ice melting may be the key in the North.

Spring is spawning season. Fishing for spawning fish is legal in many areas and should not be overlooked since it can produce some of the fastest action of the year. Crappie move into shallow water during the spawn and can be caught around shoreline cover only when they are spawning. Bass spawning beds and can be fished if it's legal in your area.

FACT

Spring comes at different times in different areas. It may happen in February in Georgia and May in the Wisconsin. Adapt to the fishing seasons where you will be fishing, and plan trips to other places to take advantage of the differences.

Hybrids, white bass, and landlocked striped bass make spawning runs up rivers and creeks, as do some other kinds of freshwater fish. Although hybrids can't reproduce, they don't know that and still respond to the instinct of their parent species. You can take advantage of these movements to catch them. Find a place where the lake or river narrows and set up there.

Trout respond to the spring by feeding actively and some species spawn when the water temperature warms. Walleye and perch become very active as soon as the ice melts or the water warms at all. Bream become more and more active as the water gets warmer in the spring, gradually increasing their feeding. And catfish start looking for more food to be ready to bed. You can take advantage of all of them.

Spring Fishing in Salt Water

Springtime brings many species of saltwater fish into rivers to spawn, and the season offers some of the best fishing of the year for striped bass. Some species of salmon come into the rivers in the spring, which is the best time to catch them. Steelhead make a spring spawning run in some areas and can be caught on light tackle and fly outfits, rather than by fishing deep and trolling.

Spring seems to come later in salt water since there is more water to warm. Spring is the beginning of the migration north by many species that spend the winter in warmer tropical waters, so be alert and ready to go if you live on the migration paths. Fish moving north in the spring may be one of the two times they are accessible to you. It's illegal in some places to go after spawning saltwater fish during the spring, so before you make a long trip, check to see what fish, if any, are protected there.

Summer Has Fishing Advantages

Summer fishing is always pictured as laid back, relaxing fishing, and it may be that way in some areas. In the South, it's almost too hot to fish during the day; most days you won't be comfortable except early and late. In the North, summer may be the best time of year to fish since it can be very short and fish usually feed actively during the short time they have. And some places on the West Coast seem to have summer all the time.

Summer Fishing in Fresh Water

In the South, try bass fishing at night; bass feed during the lower heat and light, and you will be much more comfortable while fishing for them. At night, crappie, white bass, hybrids, and stripers will all come to lights hung over the side of your boat to feed on shad attracted by the lights, making them easy to catch. And fishing at night for catfish is a tradition in many Southern states.

In Northern states, bass feed all day long to take advantage of the short growing season and you can take advantage of them. Walleye and perch bite best at night on many lakes. Muskie are active and will hit around shallow grass beds. Bream bed all summer long in most areas and you can have some fast action for them.

ALERT!

Trolling with a motor is illegal in some states so be sure to check before fishing that way. You can row and troll in most places, but doing that defeats the cooling part of trolling, although it can be a good way to catch fish and get some exercise.

Trolling is a good way to fish during the summer since you keep moving and have some breeze to cool you off. It will get your baits down deep where many fish stay in hot weather, too. Wading rivers and streams is cooling to you and puts you close to the fish, so try getting wet to beat the heat.

Summer Offers Good Saltwater Fishing

Summer is the time of party boats in most areas. Seas are usually their calmest of the year and smaller boats can venture out safely. Most fish are as spread out on their range as they get, so they can be caught in a wider variety of areas. And it's open season on almost all species.

This is a good time to go out and fill your freezer with sea bass, cod, and croaker. Although it can get extremely hot, there's usually a breeze and taking a covered boat to provide shade will keep you comfortable most days. Baitfish are easy to catch and bait shops have the best variety of bait this time of year, too.

Summer flounder are called that because they move into bays and can be caught in large numbers. Fishing from piers and bridges can be excellent for catching them. Mackerel are moving up the coast and schools sometimes come in close enough to shore to be caught from piers. Bluefish move close to shore to feed and will hit just about anything thrown to them. And fishermen with boats find many kinds of fish concentrated around offshore oil rigs and reefs.

On the Gulf Coast and southern Atlantic, redfish and sea trout are in shallow waters feeding, and these excellent table-fare fish can be caught easily. Fish for them in the shell beds with live shrimp. You'll probably also catch jack crevalle and other fish that will fight hard, but these won't be too good to eat. Just enjoy them and let them go to fight again.

Fall Is Ideal for Fishing

Fall can be one of the most beautiful times of year to fish with the colorful leaves on shoreline hardwoods setting off the edge of the lake. Fish are feeding heavily to get ready for the approaching lean winter months. Many animals are active and are enjoyable to watch, and pleasure boaters become scarce.

The shorter days of fall give you less time for fishing, especially after work, so planning becomes even more important. Most vacations are over, the kids are back in school, and you must work around their schedules if you want to take them with you.

Dressing for the weather can be difficult in the fall just as in the spring. Mornings are often almost cold while the middle of the day is very warm. Dressing in layers is the way to go because you can adjust what you're wearing easily. Just be prepared for the changing temperatures when you go.

The weather is usually calm and good early in the fall but gets progressively worse as winter approaches. Be prepared and schedule trips around weather forecasts. Going offshore for fish migrating south can be a very rewarding trip this time of year, but be sure to watch the weather and be prepared to head in.

Freshwater Fishing in Fall

Fall runs of some kinds of salmon and steelhead offer fast fishing in many streams and rivers. Bass move shallow to feed and are easier to catch in numbers then just about any other time. Walleye and perch also feed and are at their biggest and fattest of the year. Bluegill, as always, cooperate by hitting anything they see.

Saltwater Offers an Abundance of Migrating Fish

Saltwater fish that migrated north during the spring will be headed back south and pass your way again in the fall. They school up and can be caught in huge numbers when you find a group of them. As they travel, they often come in close to shore just as they do in the spring, so pier fishing can be good.

Bottom fish like grouper and sea bass will move to more shallow water as it cools in the fall, bringing them closer to shore and cutting the time it takes to run out to them. They will stay in more shallow water until near the end of the fall when the water gets really cold, and then they will move back out to deeper water for the winter.

In the late fall, the season closes for some saltwater fish, especially in the Southeast. Check local regulations before keeping fish to make sure it's not a closed season for them.

Winter Fishing Can Be Harsh in the North

If you live in southern Florida or southern California, winter is something you read about. But if you live in northern Minnesota or North Dakota, it's a numbing reality so bad you don't want to stick your nose out the door. You can still fish even under some of the worst conditions, but some winter fishing is much more comfortable than others. You also must take some safety precautions during the winter in most places.

Freshwater Fishing When the Water Gets Cold

In the winter when the water gets cold, freshwater fish slow down. At cold enough temperatures they become almost totally inactive, feeding very irregularly. Fish are cold-blooded so their body functions slow down and they just don't need as much food.

Largemouth bass get very inactive in the South when the water hits forty-five degrees, but in the North smallmouth bass may be very active at that temperature. Big bass seem to feed more in the cold water, so winter is often the best time to catch a lunker. Fish slowly to match the metabolism of the fish; offer an easy meal right in front of their face and you can catch one worth mounting.

Panfish will feed even under the ice, so fishing for them can produce some fresh fish as well as a good excuse to get out of the house in the winter. Yellow perch, bluegill, and crappie can all be caught during the coldest weather in the North and feed all winter long in the South. Walleye also feed in cold water, and winter is the best time to catch them in the southern-most parts of their range.

Northern pike are often caught through the ice and big ones seem to feed more than smaller fish. In the South, hybrid striped/white bass are active when the water is in the forties and fifties, often schooling on top chasing shad during the winter there. Catfish gather in the deepest holes in ponds and rivers in the winter and you can catch them if you present the right bait to them.

If you live in very warm climates, winter can be spawning time for fish. Bass often spawn in southern Georgia and Florida in January so you must consider the climate when talking seasons of the year. Don't think you have to fish the same way no matter where you fish; you need to adapt to local conditions. Take advantage of fishing opportunities where you live during the winter. Fish for bedding bass in Florida, or through the ice for pike in Michigan—go for whatever is available to you in the winter.

ALERT!

Hypothermia is a danger to fishermen in the winter. You can quickly lose control of your muscles in cold water so you must be extremely careful not to fall in. Wearing floatation devices at all times is even more important this time of year.

Saltwater Fishing Is Great, Depending on Where You Live

Some species of saltwater fish may winter out of your area but others may come to you this time of year. Conditions may get too bad to go fishing in the winter in northern climates, so all you can do is head south or clean tackle and wait on better weather. A winter fishing vacation to warmer beaches might be just what you need.

But don't overlook good surf-fishing and inshore fishing near you. Some kinds of saltwater fish feed actively even during the winter. Record cod and tautog have been caught in New York in January. Be very cautious of the weather when fishing waters up North in the winter.

On the West Coast, southern California waters produce big Pacific mackerel in January, and big California halibut can be taken during the winter. Giant sea bass also feed during the winter in that area, and striped bass move into bays and river mouths. Going after them in those waters would help you escape colder weather, too.

Ice Fishing

Fishing through the ice is a favorite winter pastime of many Northern anglers. You can get out of the house and spend time on the water even if it's hard on top. You can rough it fishing out in the open or you can fish from a ice shanty with all the comforts of home.

Before going out on the ice make sure it's thick enough not to be dangerous. Just because others are out there fishing doesn't mean it's safe. On big lakes, stay near the shore and don't get close to the outer edge of the ice before all the open water is gone. And be very careful taking snowmobiles and vehicles on the ice.

Cutting holes in the ice can be done with a hand or power auger, or even an ice spud (a kind of knife). Using the hand auger or spud is a good way to work up a sweat and then be really cold when you stop to fish. Some people like to cut several holes and fish them all, while others are satisfied with one hole to fish. Sitting over the hole and jigging a tiny jig or spoon, tipped with a maggot, minnow, or piece of fish, is a good way to catch fish. Tip-ups are devices that sit in the hole and pop up a flag when you get a bite, so if you set up several lines, you can watch them over a large area.

Some folks sit on a bucket on the ice beside the hole, exposed to wind and cold; others protect themselves with portable tents; and many more people build themselves ice shacks for protection. Some lakes look like small towns with all the ice shacks that stand in one spot all winter. The shacks can have all the comforts of home, from beds to stoves and televisions. Fishing in one can be just like sitting in your living room at home; that is, if your living room has a hole in the floor with water and fish in it.

Give ice fishing a try to beat cabin fever and catch some fish to eat. Just about any kind of fish in the lake can be caught under the ice, but perch and pike are most common. Check with local bait shops for tips on where to fish and what to use. And if there's a lake near you with an ice-fishing shanty town, you might find a bait shop right on the ice.

Night Fishing

Fishing at night is a good way to beat the summer heat but it can be productive at all times of the year. All kinds of fish feed at night and some feed in the dark better than they do during the day. Try fishing at night and you may open up a completely new fishing experience.

Fishing Fresh Water at Night

Sitting by a fire on the edge of a pond with several rods out for catfish is a common practice. Fishermen bait up bank hooks, trotlines, or jugs and then go back to camp and fish with rod and reel while waiting for a bite on the set hooks. A rod holder is a must because a big catfish can take your rod and reel before you can react if you let your guard down. Bait up with liver, earthworms, or live fish for nighttime cats.

Bass fishing at night is very popular in the South, and many lakes have weekly night tournaments. Anywhere it gets too hot to comfortably fish during the day is a good place to fish at night. And lakes are calmer with no skiers and pleasure boaters to bother you. Cast plastic worms, spinner baits, crank baits, or jigs to the same places that hold fish during the day. A jitterbug fished around cover is a classic way to fish top water at night. Just be prepared for heart-stopping strikes.

Tying up under a bridge, hanging a lantern over the side of the boat, and dropping minnows down to crappie, white bass, hybrids, and stripers is so common in the South that many bridges look as if they have towns under them. The lights attract small baitfish which in turn attract fish that feed on them. Any fish that eats baitfish can be caught like this at night, and it is a relaxing way to fish.

FACT

Lighted docks are good places to fish at night for the same fish that come to lights under bridges. Look for any lights near the water and try fishing around them at night from a boat or from the bank if you have access to it.

Trout fishing at night can be an excellent way to catch the biggest fish in the river or stream. Wading at night takes some getting used to and is more dangerous, but you can do it; you can also fish from the bank for nighttime trout. Use spinning equipment for live bait or small jigs and crankbaits, or use fly rods to fish flies that match the hatch of any bug out that night.

Saltwater Fishing at Night Can Be Thrilling

Fishing at night in salt water can seem like a scary thing to do, especially if you've watched some of the shark movies. Sharks do feed at night and so do most other saltwater fish, so fishing in the dark can be very productive.

Some party boats go out for reef fishing at night and produce big catches. Flounder hit good at night on flats and you can even wade and jig them in some places. Fishing where lights on docks, bridges, or piers shine on the water can be excellent, too. You can catch everything from sharks to mackerel. Snook and other saltwater fish can be caught in the shallows, and you can even cast to rising fish around those lights. Make sure you have all the bait and equipment you need since tackle stores on piers usually close up at night. Fish all night long and you'll have less company after midnight when most folks go home. Ⓔ

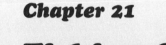

Chapter 21

Fishing Clubs and Guides

The solitude of fishing is one of the things that attract many people to the sport, but fishing with others has benefits, too. You can fish with friends or hire a guide to learn the best fishing spots and methods in your area. And joining a club gives you the chance to share time with like-minded people.

Join a Local Club

Joining a fishing club instantly gives you a group of fishermen to associate with and share knowledge and expenses with. You can find many different kinds of clubs, from those that target one species and hold tournaments for them, like bass clubs, to clubs that take trips to fish for whatever is biting at the time. Both kinds of clubs have their good and bad points, so you can chose the kind you like best—or join one of each.

Tournament Clubs

Competition has long been an integral part of fishing and many friends have made bets on first fish, biggest fish, most fish, and other catches for years. In the late 1960s Ray Scott formed the Bass Anglers Sportsman Society (BASS) and changed the way people fished. Tournament became a common way of fishing and professional bass fishermen earned a living fishing the tournament trails. Local clubs were started and federated with BASS to provide weekend bass fishermen the tournament experience.

Joining a bass club will give you access to knowledgeable bass fishermen, partners for tournaments, set times to go fishing, and a chance to try out tournament fishing. There are so many clubs in the United States that you probably aren't far from one. Most have low yearly dues and the tournaments typically cost $10 to $20 to enter. It's an inexpensive way to get started tournament bass fishing.

Walleye, striper, and catfish clubs have also been formed to fish tournaments for those species of fish. They operate in similar ways to bass clubs. There's now a professional walleye trail with prize money that rivals the bass tournaments. Joining one of these clubs gives you the same benefits as a bass club but for different kinds of fish.

You often have to join a national organization when you join a local club, but it's well worth it. You get a magazine with tips for that species as well as information about advances in equipment and technology. In fact, it's worth joining a national club even if you don't join a local one.

Many fishermen frown on tournament fishing, but it drives advances in the sport. Much of the technology and equipment developed over the past thirty years wouldn't be around if it were not for tournaments. There are many good things about tournament fishing: The tournament trails usually encourage sportsmanship; they endeavor to protect the environment; and they encourage youth to start fishing.

There are many kinds of saltwater fishing clubs, too. Some hold big tournaments for specific kinds of fish like mackerel, and others have tournaments for a variety of species. Those on the coast may have regular tournaments for members as well as open tournaments several times each year where anyone can enter. You can learn from them just as you can learn from freshwater clubs, and the other benefits are the same, too.

Sportsman Clubs

Different kinds of sportsman clubs have been around for many years. Some have regularly scheduled meetings where fishing as well as other outdoor activity information is shared. Fishing trips are scheduled for the group, and members often travel together to destinations far from home. Some even have their own land and lakes for members to use. Others have lots on big lakes where clubhouses, camping, and boat access is available to members.

Finding such a club it not as easy as finding and joining a tournament club. Sportsman clubs are often open to membership by invitation only, meaning you have to meet and get to know a member before you can join. And the expenses can be high, especially for clubs that own lakes, but access to a private lake is worth the money for many dedicated fishermen.

Clubs that fish salt water can often be found many miles from the coast. Members meet regularly and discuss tactics and equipment, and often have speakers to inform them about ways to fish, advances in equipment, or fishing opportunities. Those clubs often take several trips each year to a hot saltwater fishing spot, and the cost per member can be very reasonable when a large group goes.

National Clubs and Organizations

National groups do not offer the same opportunities as local clubs do for learning and sharing information with other members; but they do offer fishermen a lot of benefits. Joining a national organization can help you become a better fisherman and offer you ways to save money. Most publish a magazine for members that is full of helpful information. Most have some kind of program where members can get discounts on everything from fishing tackle to guide services.

Joining the International Game Fish Association (IGFA) will get you a copy of their annual record book of all fresh- and saltwater species. Become a member of BASS and get a magazine as well as free tackle each time you renew your membership. Crappie fishermen can join Crappie, USA, and get a magazine as well as crappie tournament information. The Gar Anglers Sportsman Society offers merchandise and information about gar fishing. PikeMasters offers a publication and tournaments for pike.

Saltwater fishermen would be interested in the IGFA but they also have specific organizations like the Gulf Coast Anglers Association and the Inshore Saltwater Anglers Association that offer magazines and information about those kinds of saltwater fishing. The Coastal Conservation Association has groups in every coastline state as well as the national organization. The Recreational Fishing Alliance fights to protect fresh and saltwater game fish.

ALERT!

Be wary of clubs and groups that offer something for nothing. If it sounds too good to be true, it probably is. Be careful joining groups that offer a lot of free tackle or promise that you will be a field tester for tackle you can keep.

These are just a few of the many groups you can join for information and benefits. Check with fishing friends for groups they like and consider those. Check out groups that have goals you can support and those that offer you what you need. Most will be helpful to you and well worth joining. (See Appendix A for more information on tournament groups and fishing organizations.)

Guides

Hiring a guide is a great way to catch fish on new waters, or to learn new spots and tactics on waters you already fish. Guides spend almost every day on the water looking for schools of fish and studying their habits. You can benefit from their knowledge by paying them for a trip. Consider sharing the cost with a friend to save money.

What to Expect from a Freshwater Guide

Freshwater guides usually concentrate on one species of fish or one method of fishing. Bass guides are the most common in most areas and will take you out for a half or full day of fishing. They usually provide everything you need, but welcome you using your own equipment if you want to do so. Many will share as much information about the structure where fish are holding and fish habits as you want to hear.

Muskie guides will warn you that it takes a lot of effort to hook up with one, but will give you the best chance to do so. Trout guides will help you find suitable waters and equipment to catch different species in different areas. You'll also find guides specializing in crappie, walleye, striper, or hybrid.

Some guides specialize in live-bait fishing and you can catch a wide variety of game fish with them. You can also learn how to get the bait, how to keep it alive, and the best ways to hook it, and what baitfish to look for if you come back later without a guide. And you never know what you might catch when you're fishing with live bait. Striper guides often bring in catfish and bass, and muskie guides catch pike and bass, too.

Some guides specialize in teaching you as well as helping you catch fish. They'll tell you why you're fishing a particular place, why fish are there, and what they are doing. The equipment you're using on the trip will be explained—why it's the right choice for that particular time. The guides will help you understand the fish so that after the trip you can catch them better on your own.

Saltwater Guides Are Boat Captains

Guides on salt water are usually called captains, even on small boats or when they take out only one or two fishermen at a time. They tend to be very specialized in the areas where they fish because the equipment and boats have to fit that kind of fishing. Going out on the flats for tarpon, bonefish, or redfish requires a different kind of boat than the one that takes you bottom-fishing for grouper.

Hiring a guide to take you out on the flats or for inshore fishing is a much more economical way to fish salt water unless you go often. If you live a long way from the coast and fish a few times a year, you're better off hiring someone that knows the water and has the equipment than trying to maintain your own. And you're more likely to catch fish since the guide knows what's biting and where, because the guide fishes almost every day.

ESSENTIAL

Unless you're working through a resort or hotel, check references before going out with a guide. If you hire a guide on your own, you should check with other customers to make sure you'll get what you pay for. Check ahead of time to avoid wasting your money on a bad experience.

Nobody, not even guides, can catch fish on every trip. Sometimes you may fish with a guide and have a poor day catching fish, but you can still get your money's worth if the guide explains what's going on and shows you places you can catch fish later. Some will offer another trip or a refund of part of your money if the fish just don't bite; but remember, the guide has done the job even if the fish did not do theirs. If the guide has a good reputation and you enjoy the trip, you can blame the fish, not the guide, for the lack of action. (E)

Appendix A

Getting Information about Fishing

Internet

Bass fishing:
✍ *www.wmi.org/bassfish*

Catfish fishing:
✍ *www.stormpages.com/katchaser*

Fly-fishing:
✍ *www.about-flyfishing.com*

Freshwater fishing:
✍ *http://fishing.about.com*

OutdoorFrontiers:
✍ *www.outdoorfrontiers.com*

Saltwater fishing:
✍ *http://saltfishing.about.com*

Magazines

*In-Fisherman, Walleye In-Sider, and
Catfish In-Sider Guide*
2 In-Fisherman Drive, Baxter, MN 56425
Phone: 218-829-1648

Field and Stream
2 Park Avenue, New York, NY 10016
Phone: 1-800-289-0639

Outdoor Life
P.O. Box 54733, Boulder, CO 80322
Phone: 1-800-365-1580

Game and Fish Publications
2250 Newmarket Parkway, Suite 110,
Marietta, GA 30067
Phone: 770-953-9222, ext. 2016
Individual magazines published in
twenty-eight different states

Books

Kreh, Lefty. *Fly Fishing in Salt Water.*
New York, NY: Lyons Press, 1997.

Larsen, Larry. *Larry Larsen on Bass
Tactics: How You Can Catch More and
Bigger Bass.* Lakeland, FL: Larsen's
Outdoor Publishing, 1992.

McClane, A. J. *McClane's Field Guide to
Saltwater Fishes of North America: A
Project of the Gamefish Research
Association.* New York, NY: Henry Holt
and Co., 1978.

Ross, David. *The Fisherman's Ocean.*
Mechanicsburg, PA: Stackpole Books, 2000.

Zhorne, Jeff. *The Everything® Fly-Fishing
Book.* Avon, MA: Adams Media Corporation,
1999.

Appendix B

E Glossary of Fishing Terms

A

angling: Fishing with a pole and line.

artificial bait: Any bait that's not alive and has never been alive.

B

backlash: A line tangle on a bait-casting reel caused by the spool spinning after the line has stopped going out.

bail: The pivoting U-shaped part of a fishing reel that guides the line onto the spool during rewinding.

bait spreader rig: A rig with arms with hooks at the ends and a sinker in the middle.

bait walker: A V-shaped wire with a weight on one arm; the line attaches in the V, and, on the other arm, there's a place to tie another line with a hook.

bait: Anything used to catch fish.

bait-casting reel: A reel with a revolving spool.

bait-casting rod: A rod with small guides and a grip positioned to hold the reel on top.

baitfish: Small fish that usually run in schools and are fed on by most predators.

barbless hook: A hook with no barb; required on some waters.

billy: A short heavy stick or club used to kill fish.

bobber: Same as a float.

brackish water: Water that is a mixture of salt and fresh water, usually found where freshwater rivers and streams enter the ocean.

braided line: Line that is woven from smaller fibers into a strong braid.

bream: Any sunfish including bluegill, shellcracker, redbreast, and others.

bucktail: A lead-head jig with hair, usually the tail hair of a deer, tied to it to imitate minnows.

C

casting reel: Same as a bait-casting reel.

catch and release: The practice of releasing fish after landing them so they can be caught again.

ceviche: A pickled fish made with vinegar or lime juice, peppers, and onions.

charters: Boats for rent that include a captain and usually a crew; usually found on bigger bodies of water.

chest waders: Waterproof waders that cover you from your feet to your chest, usually held up with suspenders.

chugger: A top-water bait with a concave face that makes a gurgling sound in the water when it's pulled.

closed-face reel: Same as a spin-casting reel.

copolymer line: Line made by mixing two or more kinds of materials together.

cork: Same as a float.

cradle: A special kind of landing device for long fish that looks like a small stretcher with netting or canvas between two poles.

crankbait: A plug that is reeled through the water; some have a lip that makes them wiggle and others have a body shape that makes them move like a baitfish.

creel: A wicker basket used to carry fish.

creel limit: The number of fish you can catch each day as well as the number you can have in your possession.

D

dock: A manmade structure extending out over the water for boats to tie to; usually floats on the surface of the water.

downrigger: A heavy weight on a cable that allows you to get a bait down to deep fish and keep it there while trolling.

drag: A system of washers or gears that let line slip from the reel when a fish pulls on the line.

drift-fishing: Moving baits along the bottom from a boat or by allowing currents to move them along.

dry fly: A floating fly that imitates an adult insect.

F

ferrules: Fittings on rods that allow you to put two pieces together to form one rod.

fillet: To cut meat from a fish; also the piece of meat resulting from cutting it away from the bones.

fish finder rig: A way of tying a sinker to the end of your line, with a dropper line and hook attached above it.

float: Used to hold bait above the bottom and to indicate bites when it moves; also called a bobber or a cork.

fluorocarbon lines: Line made from a special compound that is almost invisible underwater.

fresh water: Water that does not contain salt, including most lakes, rivers, and ponds.

fused line: Line made by gluing strands of fibers together and coating them with a bonding agent.

G

gaff: A big hook on the end of a handle to help you land fish.

game fish: Any fish that can be caught on hook and line, or a fish that is identified as desirable by fishermen.

gill net: A net with a large mesh designed so fish swim into it and get tangled by the gills.

guides: The devices on a rod that feed the line to the tip; also, people who take others out fishing for a fee.

H

head boat: Same as a party boat.

hip waders: Waterproof boots that come up to your hips, for wading streams and shallow rivers.

hypothermia: Subnormal body temperature, which can be caused, among other things, by wading in cold water.

I

inboard motor: A motors that sits inside the boat and has a straight shaft that runs out the back of the boat and holds the propeller.

inland waters: Waters near shore on the ocean, usually smaller and safer then the open sea.

inline spinner: A wire shaft with a spinner that rotates in front of a hook.

J

jaw spreader: A simple wire spring that holds the fish's mouth open.

jetty: An extension of the bank sticking out into the water, usually made of rock.

jig: A lead head on a hook, usually dressed with feathers, hair, or a rubber skirt; a jig is jerked up and down in the water in an action called jigging.

jon boat: A small flat-bottomed boat used for fishing protected waters.

jug fishing: A method of putting out hooks tied to a short leader and attached to a jug; after baiting them they're floated on the surface of a lake or pond.

L

landing net: A net with a handle used to help land fish.

lead: Also called a sinker, a small heavy object used to sink your bait to the bottom.

leader: A strong wire or fishing line, one end of which is tied to the hook; the other to the main line.

limb lines: Set hooks tied to a short line that is attached to tree limbs hanging over the water.

live bait: Any living critter used to catch fish.

live well: A container that is used to hold and transport live fish; it's filled with water and is often equipped with an aeration system.

M

minnow: A small fish often used as bait.

monofilament line: Fishing line made of a mixture of chemicals heated to form a gelatinlike substance that is then extruded through a small hole to form one strand of line.

N

nymphs: Artificial underwater flies that imitate immature insects.

O

offshore waters: Waters away from the shore; the open waters of the ocean.

open-faced reel: Same as a spinning reel.

outboard motor: A self-contained motor with the power head and gearing in one unit that sits on the transom of the boat.

outdrive motor: A motors that sits inside the boat but is hooked to a drive unit much like the lower half of an outboard.

outfitter: A business that rents you equipment for fishing and takes you to places to fish, but doesn't provide a guide.

outrigger: Poles off the side of the boat that spread baits in a wide pattern and allow you to use more rods while trolling.

P

panfish: Any small fish that is usually cooked whole, including bream, crappie, and perch.

party boat: A boat that takes out a large group of people for bottom fishing, for which you pay a small fee; also called a head boat.

pier: A structure over the water supported by pilings or posts.

pitching: A way of casting a bait that keeps it near the surface of the water.

plug: A three-dimensional lure that runs on top of or through the water.

pole: Any kind of fishing rod with no guides. The line is tied to the end, and the pole is used as a lever to swing the line out over the water.

popper: Same as a chugger.

popping bug: A floating fly with a concave face that makes a gurgling noise when pulled; it resembles anything from a frog to a hurt minnow.

prepared bait: Baits that fill the gap between live bait and artificial bait that are easy to carry and easy to use; some were once alive but others are things fish would never see in their natural world.

protected waters: Small waters that are not made extremely rough by wind since trees and hills block it. They can be creeks, ponds, small rivers and lakes, and inlets.

R

reel: A device for holding and retrieving fishing line.

rig: Specially prepared terminal tackle; also an outfitted boat.

riprap: Rocks placed on the bank to prevent erosion; usually found around bridges and docks.

rod blank: The fiberglass or graphite rod before guides and handles are added.

rod guide: The part of the rod the line goes through that guides the line down the rod to the tip.

rod taper: The stiffness of the rod; how much it will bend when put under pressure.

rod: The piece of fishing equipment that the reel attaches to; used to cast the line and lure.

S

salt water: Ocean water and seawater that contain salt.

scents: Substances added to lures and baits that give them a strong smell.

seine: A long net with small mesh that has a stick at each end for a person to hold while pulling it through the water to catch fish.

sensitivity: The ability of the rod to transfer vibrations to your hands.

set hooks: Hooks baited, put out, and left to catch fish without any action on the fisherman's part.

sinker: Same as a lead.

skitterpoling: A method of fishing where a short piece of line is tied to the end of a pole and a lure is fished along the surface to attract fish.

snap: A small clip used to hook lures to line.

Snelled hook: A hook tied to a leader by wrapping the line round the hook shaft, rather than tying through the hook eye.

spawn: The act of fish laying eggs and fertilizing them.

spin-casting reel: A closed-face reel with a stationary spool; the line is wound on it by a revolving cap.

spin-casting rod: A rod made for a spin-casting reel, with guides and reel seat arranged so the reel is held on the top side of the rod.

spinning reel: An open-faced reel with a stationary spool; the line is wound on it by a revolving wire bail.

spinnerbait: A V-shaped lure with a hook at one

end, revolving blades attached at the other, and a place to tie the line in the point of the V.

spinning rod: A rod designed to hold a spinning reel with big guides near the reel and smaller guides near the tip, arranged so the reel is held under the rod.

Split Shot: A small round sinker with a cut down the side where fishing line is placed; the shot is crimped on the line to hold it in place.

spoon: A metal fishing lure shaped like the bowl of a spoon with a line tie at one end and hooks at the other.

sport fishing: Trying to catch fish for the fun of the fight rather than for food.

still-fishing: Fishing while sitting still on the bank, pier, dock, or boat.

streamers: Flies that look like minnows swimming in the water.

stringer: A cord with a pointed metal shaft on one end to slip through the gills of the fish.

swivel: A device tied between the line and lure to allow the lure to rotate without twisting the line.

T

tailwaters: The waters directly below dams.

terminal tackle: Hooks, sinkers, floats, swivels, and other related items tied to the end of your line.

top-water baits: Lures fished on the surface of the water.

trash fish: Fish that are undesirable, often not good to eat and disliked by some fishermen; not all fish so labeled are considered trash fish by all fishermen.

treble hook: Three hooks fused together, usually found on fishing lures.

trolling: The act of pulling a bait through the water from a moving boat.

trotline: A long line with short dropper lines along it with hooks attached; they're stretched across a section of water, the hooks baited, and the trotline is left for fish to find.

tube bait: A round hollow soft-plastic lure with tentacles at one end.

U

ultralight: A rod or reel designed to fish very light line and lures.

W

weir: A type of fish trap consisting of a long line of poles or nets that guide fish into a small area to be held until collected.

weight: Another name for a sinker.

wet fly: A fly that has wings and looks like an adult insect underwater.

Appendix C

Species Information

Barracuda, Great

Waters where found: Saltwater reefs and shallow flats; All tropical waters except the East Pacific

Description: Cigar-shaped fish with wide tooth-filled mouth; greenish back with light belly; some dark splotches on lower half of body

Record Weight: 84 lbs. 14. oz.

Average Weight: 15–25 lbs.

Best bait: Plugs, spoons, and live bait

Bass, Largemouth

Waters where found: Freshwater shallows and reefs to 30 ft. deep or more; Originally found in the eastern U.S. but has been stocked worldwide

Description: Bullet-shaped body with wide tail and large mouth; greenish to black back with light belly; dark markings along lateral line

Record Weight: 22 lbs. 4 oz.

Average Weight: 1–3 lbs.

Best bait: Will hit a wide variety of artificial lures and live bait

Bass, Speckled Peacock

Waters where found: Freshwater rivers and streams; Orinoco and Amazon River Basins in South America; introduced to many tropical and semitropical waters worldwide

Description: Bullet-shaped body with three vertical black bars on sides; body dark green to yellow

Record Weight: 27 lbs.

Average Weight: 5–10 lbs.

Best bait: Plugs, spoons, spinners, streamers, and popping bugs, live bait.

Bluegill

Waters where found: Freshwater shallows around any kind of cover; Native to eastern U.S., introduced worldwide

Description: Wide oval-shaped body, dark blue to yellow, with a light vertical bars; round black flap just behind the gill cover

Record Weight: 4 lbs. 12 oz.

Average Weight: ¼ pound

Best bait: Small spinners and flies, live crickets, worms, and grubs

Catfish, Blue

Waters where found: Freshwater lakes, rivers, and ponds; Native to Mississippi, Missouri, and Ohio River basins; introduced throughout North America

Description: Bullet-shaped body with forked tail; spines on dorsal and lateral fins; dark blue to black back; cream-colored belly

Record Weight: 111 lbs.

Average Weight: 3–15 lbs.

Best bait: Live, prepared, and cut bait

Crappie, White

Waters where found: Freshwater lakes, streams, and rivers; Shallow slow-moving or still water with brush or weeds

Description: Oval silver body with black back; black spots arranged in 7–9 vertical bars on sides

Record Weight: 5 lbs. 3 oz.

Average Weight: ½ pound

Best bait: Live minnows and small jigs

Croaker, Atlantic

Waters where found: Saltwater shallow shell beds in bays and beach areas; East coast of North America

Description: Flattened oval silver body with black back; short black vertical bars on upper sides

Record Weight: 5 lbs. 8 oz.

Average Weight: ½ pound

Best bait: Small minnows, bloodworms, sandworms, and cut bait

Dolphin

Waters where found: Saltwater tropical and warm temperate seas in offshore deep waters; Worldwide

Description: Long bullet-shaped body with blunt head; dorsal fin runs length of body; forked tail; iridescent blue or blue-green back; gold or silvery gold on lower flanks; silvery white or yellow belly

Record Weight: 88 lbs.

Average Weight: 5–15 lbs.

Best bait: Live bait or large surface and deep-running plugs

Flounder, Summer

Waters where found: Saltwater shallows and out to 80 fathoms deep; Western Atlantic from Maine to South Carolina

Description: Flat oval body with both eyes on left side of body; dorsal and anal fin run length of back and belly; dark gray to black body with black spots; blind side is white

Record Weight: 22 lbs. 7 oz.

Average Weight: 1 pound

Best bait: Live and preserved minnows, cut bait, and small spoons and spinners

Gar, Longnose

Waters where found: Freshwater shallow bays and backwaters on rivers and lakes; Entire eastern half of U.S.

Description: Slender, round body with a long narrow beaklike mouth full of teeth; bony diamond-shaped scales; gray or dark green with black spots

Record Weight: 50 lbs. 5 oz.

Average Weight: 3–5 lbs.

Best bait: Anything that moves, but they are hard to hook because of their bony mouth

Marlin, Blue

Waters where found: Saltwater offshore open ocean; Tropical and warm temperate waters in Atlantic and Pacific Oceans

Description: Bullet-shaped with small dorsal fin, large sickle-shaped tail, and small spearlike beak; blue back; silver sides and belly

Record Weight: 1,376 lbs.

Average Weight: 150–200 lbs.

Best bait: Trolling whole live bait like bonito, dolphin, ballyhoo, and squid or large artificial tube baits, fish-shaped lures, jigs, and spoons; also big cut strip baits

Muskie

Waters where found: Freshwater shallows with weeds and rocky shorelines in lakes and rivers; Eastern U.S. and Canada from Great Lakes south to Georgia and north to Quebec

Description: Cigar-shaped body with a slightly forked tail and big toothy mouth; brown body or green with darker bars or spots

Record Weight: 67 lbs. 8 oz.

Average Weight: 8–12 lbs.

Best bait: Big live suckers and minnows, huge spinners, and 12-inch-long plugs

Perch, Yellow

Waters where found: Freshwater lakes, rivers, and streams from very shallow to very deep; Almost every U.S. state and Canadian province, more abundant in northern states and Canada

Description: Bullet-shaped yellow body with 6–8 vertical black bars on sides

Record Weight: 4 lbs. 3 oz.

Average Weight: 4–12 oz.

Best bait: Almost any small spoon or jig, any small live bait or prepared bait, cut bait

Pike, Northern

Waters where found: Freshwater bays and shallows with weeds and other cover; Northern or Arctic waters around the world

Description: Cigar-shaped dark green or yellowish sides with lighter-colored horizontal spots or streaks; big toothy mouth

Record Weight: 55 lbs. 1 oz.

Average Weight: 2–5 lbs.

Best bait: Live minnows, flashy spinners, spoons, plugs

Snook

Waters where found: Saltwater tropics and subtropics, shallow coastal waters; North and South America, Pacific and Atlantic coasts

Description: Silver-sided cigar-shaped body; pronounced black lateral line through the tail; dark back

Record Weight: 53 lbs. 10 oz.

Average Weight: 5–10 lbs.

Best bait: Live minnows, shrimp, and crabs, artificial baits like jigs and spoons

Swordfish

Waters where found: Saltwater open ocean with depths of 400–500 fathoms or more; Tropic and temperate waters worldwide

Description: Bullet-shaped body with long dorsal and pectoral fins; sickle-shaped tail; long sword-shaped bill; dark back with lighter sides and belly

Record Weight: 1,182 lbs.

Average Weight: 100–300 lbs.

Best bait: Large trolled baits or prepared squid, live fish

Tarpon

Waters where found: Saltwater coastal waters; Atlantic temperate and subtropical waters

Description: Silver bullet-shaped body with dark back; large mouth; sickle-shaped tail; lower jaw juts out

Record Weight: 283 lbs.

Average Weight: 50–100 lbs.

Best bait: Live mullet, crabs, and shrimp, artificial spoons, plugs, and jigs

Trout, Lake

Waters where found: Freshwater deep lakes; Canada, Alaska, and the Great Lakes; introduced into other northern lakes

Description: Bullet-shaped body; fins have white leading edges and light-colored spots on a dark gray to brown body

Record Weight: 72 lbs.

Average Weight: 15–30 lbs.

Best bait: Live minnows, spoons, and plugs; trolled with downriggers

Trout, Rainbow

Waters where found: Freshwater streams and lakes; Native to west coast of North America from Alaska to Mexico; introduced extensively in cooler streams and lakes worldwide

Description: Bullet-shaped silver-gray body with colorful spots and a pink stripe down lateral line

Record Weight: 42 lbs. 2 oz.

Average Weight: 1–2 lbs.

Best bait: Flies of all kinds, small spinners and spoons, live minnows, and insects

Tuna, Bluefin

Waters where found: Saltwater open seas; Subtropical and temperate waters of the north Pacific and Atlantic Oceans

Description: Teardrop-shaped body with sickle-shaped tail and short fins; dark blue back; silver sides and belly

Record Weight: 1,496 lbs.

Average Weight: 50–300 lbs.

Best bait: Trolling or still-fishing with large live baitfish or squid, spoons, and plugs

Walleye

Waters where found: Freshwater lakes and rivers; Most of Canada and the U.S. in cooler waters; introduced widely

Description: Cigar-shaped brown body with splotches of darker color; large dorsal fins; large glassy eyes

Record Weight: 25 lbs.

Average Weight: 1–3 lbs.

Best bait: Small minnows and leaches, jigs and spoons

E Index